The
Perfect
System
of Parenting

The Perfect System of Parenting

Syd and Ellen Kessler

Foreword by Jacob and Isaac Kessler

The Perfect System of Parenting
Copyright © 2008 by Syd and Ellen Kessler

All rights reserved. No part of this publication may be reproduced or transmitted in any form or by any means, electronic or mechanical, including photocopying, recording, or any information storage and retrieval system, without permission in writing from the publisher.

First published in paperback, ePub and ePDF in 2008 by BPS Books,
a division of Bastian Publishing Services.

Published in paperback and ePub in 2019
by Kinetics Design, KDbooks.

kdbooks.ca

ISBN 978-0-978-4402-7-5 (paperback)

ISBN 978-1-988360-34-8 (ePub)

Cover design: Angel Guerra, Archetype
Text design: Tannice Goddard, Soul Oasis Networking

To our parents:
Hy and Celia Kessler
Charlie and Helen Duplain
Rav and Karen Berg

To our children:
Jacob and Isaac Kessler

This book could not have been made without the genius, compassion, and vision of Don Bastian and Su Bundock.

Contents

Foreword ix

Introduction 1

Part 1 / Learning the System 9
  1 The Origins of the Perfect System   11
  2 What Is the Perfect System?   15

Part 2 / Working the System
  3 The Real Meaning of Parental Love   31
  4 The Rules of Parenting   41

Part 3 / The System Through the Ages and Stages
  5 Up to Age 3   57
  6 From 3 to 5 Years   71

7	From 6 to 9	79
8	From 10 to 13	95
9	14 and Beyond	105

Conclusion	113
For Further Reading	115

Foreword

Jacob:

As this book was being put together, someone came up with the bright idea of having the authors' children write the foreword. At first I wasn't so sure about this. After all, I am not the most objective person to validate a book on parenting written by my parents. But then again, who better to give testimony to the practicality of their principles?

From my point of view, their system of parenting has been put into action successfully.

What does success mean? Well, consider that I grew up in a household filled with love and appreciation. A household where my thoughts and feelings were always respected. Mom and Dad ran a tight ship, but my brother and I always knew where we were and where we were going. The journey had strict rules and guidelines, but that was always OK with us.

I know I will make many mistakes as I follow my own life path. I know I will experience both blessings and hardships. But I also know that the basic tools my parents imparted to me — in particular the principle of being a cause and not an effect — will assist me in righting myself and will elevate all of my experiences.

My parents have been working on this book for several years but waited to publish it until Isaac and I were adults. They were concerned about the spotlight that the book would shine on us. I am now 25 and Isaac is 23. I am prepared to be scrutinized. It is the least I can do to show my gratitude to my parents.

Thank you, Mom and Dad.

Isaac:

I have found it very difficult to contribute to this foreword. Just knowing that the title of the book was *The Perfect System of Parenting* caused my hands to seize up above my computer keyboard.

How do I validate for you that these tools have moulded me for the better? I can only give you a word that is not mentioned in the text: *certainty*. It is the single most important thing that the authors of this book have shared with me: the all-encompassing understanding and personal application of certainty in my life. Certainty in my actions toward others, certainty in the life decisions I choose to make, certainty in relationships, certainty in the love I have for my family and that they have for me, certainty that if I follow the guidelines imparted to me by my parents, I will be on a path toward long-lasting fulfillment for myself and everyone around me. And lastly, certainty in myself.

I have been through pain and heartache in my relatively short life. However, my parents, through their unconditional love and support and the tools explained in this book, have given me the power to convert the pain into meaningful experiences. Growing up with them, no stone of experience was ever left unturned, and every hurt was turned to gold.

You may call my words presumptuous, egotistical, or full of chutzpah. Nevertheless, I stand by my inner wellspring of certainty and say to you that this book will definitely strengthen and improve the lives of both you and your children.

Introduction

As we parents search for help in raising our children, we are barraged by conflicting and constantly changing "wisdom" from experts, whether in articles and books or on TV, radio, and the Web. In our struggle to balance our multiple responsibilities, we are tempted to latch onto today's quick fix, ignoring the thunderclouds that are gathering in strength for tomorrow.

But this is to go into a reactive parenting mode. The result? We set off a negative chain of events, creating further disorder and disarray in our own lives and the lives of our children.

It does not have to be this way.

Allow us to tell about an early experience in our lives as parents, and how it led to this book.

When Ellen was pregnant with our first son, Jacob, we decided to write two wish lists: the first was a list of what we wanted for our new child and the second was a list of what we hoped for ourselves as we raised our new child. If this exercise revealed conflicts between the two columns, we could clear them up before active parenting duty began. We defined successful parenting as the ability to execute the wishes on both lists.

Our primary guide in making our lists was our understanding of what we call the Perfect System. This system, which will be described in more detail in chapters 1 and 2, is the foundation of our advice to you throughout this book.

Here's what we put on our first list:

What we wish for our child
- To be a happy child.
- To learn to take responsibility for his or her actions.
- To be a kind and sharing person.
- To always give the maximum effort to whatever he or she chooses to do.
- To achieve his or her ultimate potential.
- To understand that a bad action does not make him or her a bad person, just a good person who has done a bad thing.
- To love and respect nature and Mother Earth.
- To realize his or her uniqueness and to celebrate that uniqueness and the uniqueness of others as representing each person's special genius.
- To understand that all men and women have equal rights.
- To have a lifelong joy of learning.
- To ensure personal fulfillment by putting others before self.

We recognized that the last wish was potentially dangerous and damaging, since it could leave our child vulnerable to uncaring and unscrupulous people. However, the concept was essential and had to be included because of an underlying truth of the Perfect System: that the only way to get fulfillment is to first give it. In scientific terms, it is Newton's third law: For every action there is an equal and opposite reaction.

And here's what we put on our second list:

What we wish for ourselves while raising our child
- Never to be held hostage by our child's misbehaviour.
- To spend maximum and valued time with our child.
- Whenever possible to take our child with us to cultural events (movies, concerts, plays, etc.).
- To have our child experience our friends by physically being in their presence.
- With discretion, to have our child share in our total life experience.
- To be always aware that there are no bad children, only bad actions.
- To have as little crying and as much laughter as possible.
- To make the act of parenting a fulfilling experience.
- To prepare our child for a future that might not include us.

These lists were created by a 36-year-old man and a 32-year-old woman who both wanted a child at this time in their lives. Both of us were prepared to be teachers, mentors, guardians, and shepherds to that child. We were the team that was going to prepare our child for the future. We recognized from the outset that our time was limited and our task was great.

Introduction

As it turned out, we didn't come up with any conflicts between the lists. But we did find more complexity to our task than we had anticipated.

At first we felt intimidated. Our menu of goodies was grandiose. Could we deliver all of the items on our wish lists? Did we have the knowledge, ability, and tools to do so?

We started reading furiously. Only a few parenting books yielded tips and clues suited to our point of view. Our needs were so diverse that a lot of the material we gleaned cancelled itself out. Suggestions that may have served some objectives on our list would have undermined others. We were faced with a great problem, but also a great opportunity. We were forced to take knowledge from the Perfect System and morph it to fit the task at hand. The Perfect System was working as a valued tool in our personal and business relationships. Why wouldn't it be just as effective in our relationship with our child?

This book represents what we came up with. In it we share with you key principles of the system, to help you first of all as a person and then as a parent. Then we show you how to "work the system" in your family, and how to "customize" its truths to fit your children during their various ages and stages. Although the fundamental truths of parenting remain the same, the techniques of parenting have to be adjusted to meet children's different challenges and needs as they move toward maturity.

We have used the Perfect System in raising our two boys. For us, the outcome has been spectacular. At this writing, our two sons, Jacob and Isaac, are delightful young adults. They are kind and generous, sensitive and empathetic, caring and sharing. They were a pleasure to be with all through their growing up years. There were no tears or raised voices in our house, only laughter and smart conversation. This outcome was not a fluke. We didn't get lucky as parents. We were armed and ready to create this result. We mitigated our risk of failure when we turned to and trusted the rules of the Perfect System.

You could say that our outcome was predictable, because the methods and techniques we used to raise our children were perfect. They are perfect because the laws of the Perfect System are perfect. This is not a statement of arrogance. It is a statement of fact. The physical laws of the universe (the Perfect System) are irrefutable and so in their very essence are perfect.

We believe that the Perfect System will give you the insights and tools you need to develop, and celebrate, harmony and order in your family's life.

An Important Note to Single and Divorced Parents

For various reasons you may be bringing up your child alone. Although we address you throughout this book as "we" — a husband and wife — we do not want you to assume that we see every family and every situation as the same as ours. We are aware of your unique challenges.

Single parents

The information in this book about raising a child from birth to age five still holds true in situations where a spouse has died. The challenge for you will be consistency, monitoring, and informing other caregivers (relatives, nannies, etc.) to follow the principles in the book. There should not be any compromise on your part as a single parent or on the part of the caregiver.

Introduction

Single parents must be aware, however, that their wishes will not be followed to the same consistent and strict degree by other caregivers. They will have to take this into consideration and continue to monitor to pick up situations when others are putting the "game plan" at risk. Teaching the Perfect System is difficult if the caregiver does not see the need for its principles. Frankly, being a teacher, mentor, and guardian of our children's trust is a full-time commitment. At times it's a pain in the butt. It takes great commitment, concentration, and will to secure their future. Sometimes, we and the caregiver are just too tired or overwhelmed to push back at the child and so we "give in" to inappropriate behavior.

Keep in mind that the Perfect System thrives on consistency and focus. The greater the focus, the harder the work — until eventually it will become easier and easier for you to apply the principles. When you or the caregiver gives in, it will take that much longer for your child to be consistently pleasant to be around.

Divorced parents

In the category of divorced parents there are parents who cannot live together but who put their children before their personal difficulties. The information in this book, which is aimed at the normative two-parent child, works well in this kind of arrangement. It takes the same intensity of communication between the divorced parents to get the Perfect System right.

Unfortunately, there are divorces in which one parent uses the children as pawns in a "get even/revenge" chess game. This is *the* most difficult situation for any parent who wants to follow the guidelines of the Perfect System of Parenting. Not only does one of the parents treat the children as pawns, but he or she will do everything possible to denigrate the Perfect System's methodology

— not out of disagreement with it, but simply to be antagonistic to their former spouse.

The only advice we can give to the parent in this situation who wishes to follow the Perfect System of Parenting is to always take the high road. We get what we give. Let the acrimonious other parent do their shtick. In the end, children intuitively know the truth and they will subconsciously migrate to the source of love coming from the more "evenly" loving parent.

Kids understand that "giving in" isn't the same as "love." Kids thrive on order and consistency. Rules mean safety, which is a component of love. Rules mean that the parent cares so much for the child that he or she is putting these "fences" of protection around them. In the end, the fences make them feel more secure.

There is another reason to take the high road. Everything is a life lesson for our children. Children follow our example and will learn from us how to behave in similar situations as they are growing up: everything from a close friend who suddenly turns on them, to their first romantic interest, to finding their own future spouses. We must teach our children that good actions get good actions back. Bad actions get bad actions back. Our children are continually monitoring our behaviour. We are their example of what is permissible. We are the main source of influence on them. Why should they behave in an appropriate manner if we don't? It is counter-intuitive to them.

This system of parenting is therefore not just for children in these tough situations but also for the betterment of the sometimes difficult lives of their parents.

PART 1

Learning the System

1

The Origins of the Perfect System

The Perfect System, and a book of the same name,[1] are the result of my (Syd's) long search to make sense of my own life. This book, *The Perfect System of Parenting*, is a result of our application of these findings to family life. We believe that the same principles that helped us will become essential to you in your quest to become successful parents. A famous comedian once said, "I finally stopped dating because I couldn't bear to hear my life story one more time." I will not repeat my story here, just the parts that are most pertinent to our purpose.

While still in my 30s, I had risen far from my working-class roots to become a millionaire many times over. I was ensconced at the very top of North America's advertising hierarchy. To the outside

---

[1] Available from your library or through our website, www.theperfectsystem.com.

world, I was rich, powerful, and determined, driving a corporate empire with $350 million in annual revenue. I was the very epitome of the poor kid making good.

Inside, however, an emptiness was taking hold. Despite all my supposed success, I did not feel satisfied, fulfilled, or in control of my days or my life. On the contrary, I felt pushed along by outside currents. I spent my days juggling the random and unpredictable. I suffered from constant anxiety, frustration, and unhappiness. I knew that the power that I had attained was "given" by others; it was not personal power and could be taken away at any time. I was not at peace with myself, and one day I fell seriously ill.

In the dark days of my illness and long convalescence, I asked myself: Why is all this mayhem happening to me? Why do I feel a victim of events? What is it that I really want? What should I do next?

Being a linear, logical thinker, I turned to science for help. My journey led to a unique, largely undiscovered treasure chest of wisdom, a strongbox filled with functional truths together with the tools to implement those truths. It was a new way of looking at the world I lived, played, and worked in.

And it all stemmed from the universal principle of Cause and Effect.

The Perfect System proved to have within it all that was necessary to become the ultimate instruction manual for life. The wisdom of the Perfect System allowed me to understand why I had landed in the hospital in the first place and what I needed to do to accelerate my recovery. I came to understand that I had created my illness and went on to understand how to create my recovery.

Ultimately, all of this led to a new way of living that was to prove full of wonder and joy for me — and ultimately for my wife, Ellen, and the children we were to raise.

The life-jolting discovery for me was that these perfect laws and rules of the physical universe around us also apply to us — because we are all part of the same physical universe.

For now, as we conclude this chapter, consider just the main principle — the main tool — that is going to transform your parenting and your family.

Cause and Effect

The Law of Causality states that to every event there can be ascribed a cause — with the exception of the First Cause. It observes that, at one level in our physical world, nothing happens randomly. Whether we are talking about a tree, an ocean, a corporate executive, or our children, the same laws apply: for every effect, there is a cause. This is hard science, not mysticism. It is embodied in Newton's third law of motion, which states that forces always occur in pairs — that for every action there is an equal and opposite reaction.

Failure to grasp the Law of Cause and Effect creates chaos, in our lives and in our world. Full comprehension of the law is the prime determining factor in our ability to satisfy not only our personal needs and desires but also the needs and desires of our children.

Master this principle and you will begin the process of mastering your life, because the Law of Causality applies immutably to all physical matter.

If all parents taught children that causes and effects are joined, we wouldn't need elementary school courses with names like "Random Acts of Kindness," "Peacemaking," and "Conflict Resolution." We would focus on keeping the peace rather than on moderating conflict. Education in causality would eventually eradicate the need for intercession by removing the cause of conflict at its root.

And the message is so simple:

> *For every action there is an equal and opposite reaction.*

In the physical world this law never varies. It is indisputable. Its corollaries are:

- Negative actions beget negative reactions.
- Positive actions beget positive reactions.
- Therefore we are responsible for almost everything that happens to us.

2

What Is the Perfect System?

Good parenting requires that parents be whole and see the world whole.

This chapter's description of the Perfect System focuses on you as a person and your view of your task as a parent. It will help you become the parent you want to be.

The First Cause

> We are inextricably joined to everything that came before us, to all that we emerged from. We all have an affinity with the First Cause.

There are two principles at play here. The first is the inerrant Law of Causality, which states that to every event, there can be ascribed a cause, with the exception of the First Cause. The second principle is embedded in the scientifically proven laws of heredity and genetics, first identified in the 1870s by Gregor Mendel: that all living things or organisms contain traits that are passed down from parent to offspring. Mendelism has become the generally accepted theory of heredity, forming the basis of all modern genetics.

Subsequent studies in the twentieth century — most famously in the Minnesota Study of Identical Twins Reared Apart, conducted from 1979 to 1999 — proved that such hereditary traits include personality characteristics. In this study, researchers at the prestigious University of Minnesota, led by Thomas Bouchard, proved that identical twins raised apart were as alike in personality as identical twins who grew up together.

> *Our genes hold personality characteristics that are passed from generation to generation.*

This means that we all have in us a part of our parents, their parents, their parents' parents, and so on. We could trace our ancestry and basic human traits back not just to our ancient ancestors — the monkey or Adam, depending on your belief system — but to the First Cause, the Big Bang. This event was the origin of all humankind.

In the beginning this was a hard concept for me (Syd) to swallow. I felt comfortable with the Adam or monkey legacy and the arguments on either side. But after much thought I realized, with excitement, the magnitude and mystery of the idea that was ultimately underlying both: that we all come from star dust. I soon recognized that I needed a better understanding of the characteristics of this First Cause to better understand myself and the people around me.

Big Bang

Here's what science says about the First Cause, or the Big Bang. Physics verifies that in the beginning there was no physicality. There was merely an unknown energy. At some stage, for an as yet undiscovered reason, all the energy became isolated to one point, compressed into something smaller than one-trillionth the size of the head of a pin. That one point was by its essence, singularity. This state was before Time, Space, or Motion — there was no lack, no movement, only absolute completeness. There was no need, only total fulfillment.

> *We all have an affinity to the completeness of the First Cause. It is in our physical genes.*

Science tells us that this singularity, this totality, then exploded outward. It was a burst of "out-giving" that kept on giving and kept nothing back for itself. All of reality was filled — it was totally and absolutely complete. After the explosion cooled and anti-matter and matter were formed, matter, again for still undiscovered reasons, became the dominant force and, *voilà*, physicality was born. This singularity was where we all come from. It was our great, great, great, great, great, great, great-grandparent. And as we know from the law of Mendelism and subsequent genetic studies, we all have the characteristics of this grandparent.

Validation of this notion of affinity may also be found in the New Physics, which postulates that the whole universe and everything in it, regardless of distance or dissimilarity, are all integrally connected and have emanated from a single source.

Fulfillment

Everything we do is driven by our affinity with the First Cause and our need to be like it. The First Cause is the basic influencer of all of our transactions, whether social or commercial. It is the prime driver regarding the friends we pick, the brands we buy, and the parents we become.

> *More than anything else in life, we seek true, long-lasting fulfillment because – linked to the First Cause as we are – that is our nature.*

Parenting really comes into focus at this point. We all need and want fulfillment, because it is an inherent part of our affinity with the First Cause. Yet most of us are in absolute ignorance of this truth. We imagine that material things will bring happiness, so we become motivated to acquire physical objects when the opposite should be our goal. Material things will never satisfy us.

Haven't we all thought, at some point in our lives, that another car or a different mate or more clothes would bring us happiness? Surely more money would fix everything! But if any of you have managed to get all or some of these, you now know that it wasn't really true. You weren't any happier. It was just the same old you with a new mate, more money, or another car. As it is often said, no matter where you go, there you are.

You buy a car. You really want this car. What happens a week later? The satisfaction never lives up to the expectation. That's because you didn't really crave the car; you craved the way you thought the car would make you feel. Others turn to drugs, sex, or shopping sprees in their search for fulfillment. Unfortunately, these feel good at the time, but they represent *short-term* fulfillment, and we are driven to keep the feeling going. Short-term solutions unfortunately lead to guilt, emotional and physical pain, and more feelings of emptiness.

Once we understand that what we want in life is not money or physical objects but long-term, lasting fulfillment, we can take advantage of the many opportunities for true sustainable fulfillment that exist in our lives. This is no simple task. After all, the hardest thing to do is to identify in the thick of an experience why we are in that experience in the first place.

This is where a principal truth of parenting comes in. Many of us seek to satisfy our lack of fulfillment by creating children in our own likeness, hoping they will achieve or possess what we feel is lacking within ourselves. Or worse, we use our children as our personal, primary source of fulfillment. This is a treacherous path to tread.

In contrast, there is immense positive power in recognizing that:

> *The role of parents is not to seek fulfillment from their children, but to create genuine fulfillment within their children.*

Kahlil Gibran states this concept beautifully in his book *The Prophet*:

Your children are not your children,
They are the sons and daughters of Life's longing for itself,
They come through you but not from you,
And though they are with you, yet they belong not to you.

You may give them your love but not your thoughts,
For they have their own thoughts.
You may house their bodies but not their souls,
For their souls dwell in the house of tomorrow, which you cannot visit, not even in your dreams.
You may strive to be like them, but seek not to make them like you.
For life goes not backward nor tarries with yesterday.

For many of us, the decision to have children was originally part of our quest for fulfillment. We believed that children would magically make us feel complete and fill in all the blanks of our own lives. If this was the case for you, it is essential to recognize the futility of such a belief. Your role as a parent is not to seek fulfillment from your children, but to create fulfillment within your children.

> Getting love from our children should not be our prime intention.

The backdrop to this role is a great irony: that the only way to get fulfillment is to focus not on our own needs but on creating fulfillment in others — in this case, our children. Giving is one of the genuine paths toward long-lasting fulfillment. The reasons, as usual, are straightforward: the more you give, the more you must get (for every action, there is an equal and opposite reaction). And the more we give, the more affinity we have to the First Cause, the very essence of "out-giving." And the more affinity we have to it, the more fulfilled we are.

Cause and Effect

For every action, there is an equal and opposite reaction. It is that simple. And it is scientifically proven in Newton's third law of motion that forces always occur in pairs.

> *Positive actions produce positive reactions.*
> *Negative actions produce negative reactions.*
> *You are responsible for almost everything that happens to you.*

To master Cause and Effect is to begin mastering your life — and the lives of your children.

> *This principle of action-reaction is one of the fundamental truths of the Perfect System.*

Nothing less than the total comprehension of this truth will suffice. It is the essential tool of successful parenting. Babies learn from Day One: I cry ... you come. Tots learn: I smile ... you respond positively. Older kids learn: I behave in a positive manner ... positive things happen to me. And vice versa.

There can be no debate about this — causality is a law of the universe. Teach your children this critical concept and you will be doing them an immense favour. Every action has a consequence. The nature of their actions will determine whether their lives are full of positive or negative consequences. It is simple and it is fact. Children recognize this. They grasp the concept and respond to it. Cause and Effect.

Yet this important concept is easily forgotten. It is never truly taught to parents. Even worse, it is not taught to our children at any level of their education, not in their elementary, secondary, graduate, or postgraduate classrooms. There simply is no class in the world called "Cause and Effect." Yet this principle, or rather our lack of understanding this principle, has led us to wage war against our fellow beings for all of recorded history. It has also resulted in our tacit acceptance of the planet's ecological desecration. And, on the personal level, it is directly responsible for the unhappiness, disorder, and discontent of our lives.

Why do we forget the importance of Cause and Effect?

We slip into causality amnesia because no personal gain or loss is immediately evident to us in our actions. That is to say, we don't perceive any cause and effect in them. We don't see the eventual reward or consequence as tied to the action, because time separates the cause and the effect, creating an illusion that the two are not joined. Think about it: If you were to understand the effects of an action or cause (the reward or the consequence), then you would be more likely to choose positive actions over negative ones. In fact, you'd be crazy not to.

There's another reason this most fundamental of human contracts has gone by the wayside. We live in a world boiling over with examples of people, many of them in high places, who violate this principle with impunity. Some of them literally get away with murder. Others cheat on their income taxes, through loopholes or legal cunning. They don't regard their actions as serious, let alone as fraud or the abrogation of social responsibility. Many of us, in many ways, steal from each other. Many of us mentally and physically abuse our spouses and children. And there is constant injustice in the workplace. Just think of the exploitation of minds and bodies that is directly related to the ever-widening and deeply-worrying gulf between rich and poor. Daily we see all this reported in the newspapers; we witness much of it happening live on TV; and we experience it in the often tragic human dramas played out by neighbours, friends, relatives, and even ourselves.

We live in a world where choosing for ourselves without regard for others is rewarded and often applauded. We live in a "front page" world where negative behaviour and its perpetrators are not vilified but placed in the pantheon of celebrity. Actors, athletes, filmmakers, even people who are famous merely for being famous, have become our gods. Fame and notoriety are now seen as the same thing.

"News" is bad news. The media relegate any good news — any positive achievements — to the back pages. They present a distorted, short-term view of events. Their purpose is to sell programs or newspapers, which in turn sell advertising, the cost of which is determined by audience or circulation figures. It is instant gratification or nothing, these days, and any exceptions prove the rule.

We know the faces of these people we idolize, and we think we know their stories. However, as I (Syd) found out the hard way, fame and riches are in no way akin to fulfillment. In fact, no matter how successful they may appear to be, individuals who have created their fame or wealth through negative actions are irrefutably marked by disharmony, emptiness, and lack of fulfillment.

But we do not see this. We do not see the cause and effect. We do not look more closely, uncovering the personal disorder, unhappiness, and discontent that characterize so many lives — often including our own.

What would happen if we as a society were to expand our list of what is valuable in human endeavour? What if we included such positive traits as sharing, kindness, empathy, and tolerance? The answer is simple: We would cause an effect of momentous proportions. This would be a "shot heard round the world." If we lived our lives — and taught our children to live theirs — on the basis that causes and effects are joined, just imagine ... the whole world could find peace and satisfaction.

A parent's choice: be a "cause" or an "effect"

One of your primary tasks as a parent is to understand the negative and harmful repercussions of going into reactive mode (becoming an effect), and to demonstrate to your children that you take full responsibility for your actions.

Imagine that after a really hard day at the office you walk through your front door to a house full of screaming, hyperactive kids all demanding your attention. They don't care about what you've been going through and how you're feeling. They care only about what they're doing right now and how they're feeling.

How does this make you feel? Put upon? Upset? Out of control?

At the moment of impact, you probably feel like a victim. As already discussed, our affinity with the First Cause makes us hate being treated as mere objects that are acted on or that just react to the actions of others. We don't like it when things are done to us. It makes us feel alienated. This induces systemic uncertainty and a sense of being out of control.

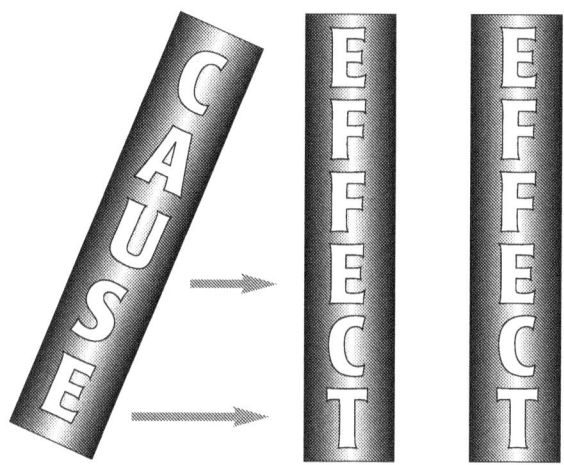

This can be explained using the time-honoured illustration of dominoes and their famous effect. When the "cause" domino falls on us (the first "effect" domino), it is painful and makes us feel out of control, put upon, abused. What often exacerbates the pain of these situations is that we are not expecting the sheer force of the cause's impact. We don't like the sudden realization that we are an object, not an actor. We don't like it because, fundamentally, part of us is like the First Cause.

But there's a hidden truth embodied in the middle domino. This middle domino has the innate potential to be both an effect and a cause. That's the secret: Every action we take has the potential to be either a cause or an effect. We simply have to be aware at all times that we have the choice.

Just consider moments in your past or everyday life when you have been an effect and not a cause. Write a list of such situations from the past week or month in a notebook. Most of the items on your list will no doubt reflect those discomforting moments, in situations both private and professional, when you should have been securely at the helm but instead weren't even on deck.

Now let's go back to the screaming, hyperactive kids. What do you do? Shriek at them to leave you alone and barricade yourself in your room? Give in to their demands? Distract them somehow? Take control? Your choice will determine whether or not you will be a cause or an effect.

- If you shriek and barricade yourself, you will continue to be an effect, for this is clearly a reaction to the kids' behaviour. Consequently, you will continue to feel like the "victim" who innocently walked through the door. What's more, the children's behaviour is going to get worse. The entire negative situation will be compounded. You have set in motion the proverbial downward spiral.
- If you take positive control of the situation and move the children into positive actions, you will become a cause rather than an effect. You will be in charge and able to feel positive emotions. You will have lived out your affinity with the First Cause. You will have actualized a basic human right and need. Furthermore, your children's behaviour will improve when they understand that the correct person is in control. A positive situation will be created and compounded. (We discuss this further, and

give examples of how to create this outcome, later in the book.)

For every action there is an equal and opposite reaction. Science surrounds this issue like Indians circling covered wagons in a bad B movie. There is no escape from this truth.

We keep pushing this point because the Law of Cause and Effect is the prime determining factor of our ability to satisfy not only our personal needs and desires, but also the needs and desires of our children.

As you understand that you need long-lasting fulfillment, and that behaviour acknowledging Cause and Effect will fill this need, you are well on your way to all the wondrous joys of family life.

Part 2

Working the System

3

The Real Meaning of Parental Love

Why did you have a child? Did you need another source of love? Did you need someone to give love to? Or was it that you and your partner wanted a physical symbol of your union with whom to share your love? We have said it before and we will say it again, because it is a critical message:

> *Giving love and getting love from our children should not be our primary intent.*

We'll go further and say that an erroneous focus on giving love to our children leads many of us into a dangerous parenting trap. As parents, we are inclined to think that the more we give in to our children's wishes, the more love we are giving them and the more they will love us back, gaining us the fulfillment we seek. However, this is actually to want something for ourselves (fulfillment), rather than to see what is best for our children (their ultimate fulfillment).

In our experience, the more permissively parents treat their children at a young age, the more likely those children are to distance themselves from their parents as they mature. Permissiveness does not build continuous, close, intimate relationships with our kids. Quite the opposite — it pushes them away.

Watch Out for the Love Ambush

Children know how to leverage our feeling for them. They know how to ambush us with a guilt-inducing "You don't love me anymore" or "I don't love you anymore" — thereby subverting our parental training. How does this happen?

> *Giving in to the "love ambush" is a key source of failure. To parent effectively, we must never surrender to this negative interaction.*

Always giving in to your child's demands is not the way to produce a positive effect. When you're seeking your children's love for your own fulfillment, only bad stuff can happen to you and eventually to your child. This is a trick we continually play on ourselves, and it can become a negative spiral. By carefully examining the situation you are in, you'll see that the problem may be that you are going against everything that the Perfect System stands for.

The following is a good example of saying no. Your four-year-old son wants a piece of chocolate cake, but you know that it will spoil his dinner. So saying no is actually best for him. But he will use every weapon in his arsenal to satisfy that craving. If all else fails, he will pull out the ultimate emotional dagger to the heart: "I don't love you any more." So it will always be easier for you to say yes. However, the best thing you can do for your son, rather than for yourself, is to still say no. He may not love you at that moment, but by saying no, you are fulfilling your job as the guardian of his body and consciousness.

> *Always ask the question: What good will my next action do for my child? If it will do no good for your child, then that's what you'll eventually get back: no good.*

Remember this key message the next time your child is begging and pleading to be allowed another cookie, an extra hour of TV, an extended curfew for a date — you fill in the blank. It is much easier to say no when you are consciously aware that this action will be best for your child and will do your child far more good than a yes.

All of which leads us to a key question.

Do We Really Love Our Children?

Wait — don't answer this loaded question until we have defined what we mean by the word "love."

As stated in my (Syd's) previous book, the Perfect System defines love as an unconditional acceptance of another person — to protect, care for, put before ourselves that person, no matter what he or she does. Total sharing. This condition is one of the prime characteristics of the Big Bang. First there was a singularity. Then there was an explosion outward. It was a burst of "out-giving" that kept on giving and held nothing back for itself. Love, in this context, is a deed and not an emotion.

What Do Our Children Need Most?

Our children are no different from us. They have an innate desire to feel filled. You know by now that the Perfect System defines this as feeling fulfilled.

Young children do not know how to create this lasting fulfillment for themselves. They are also unaware of the Law of Cause and Effect. Depending on their age, they may not even know the difference between right and wrong. And most importantly, they do not know how to protect themselves from the physical dangers that surround them.

> We are our children's guardians until they reach an age of recognition of and respect for the Law of Cause and Effect.

These facts put an enormous amount of responsibility on our shoulders. Because we do understand the Law of Cause and Effect and its connection to fulfillment, we are totally responsible for our children's well-being, intellectually, emotionally, and physically.

Any neglect of our responsibility puts our children in harm's way. We see this demonstrated all the time. Children run out into traffic chasing a ball. They touch a hot stove element or indiscriminately play with sharp objects. It's true that this is how they learn the big picture: by discovery, testing, and invention. But thankfully, they also learn this, in their early years, by our *preventing* these things from happening to them. We must protect our children from the randomness of the universe until they reach the elemental level of consciousness of the big picture. They are truly innocent victims because they are not able to perceive the ultimate blend of Cause and Effect and randomness. They don't have the tools to predetermine an outcome the way we do. As parents, we are guardians of their bodies and consciousness. This is why we believe we have absolute responsibility to teach them the concept of Cause and Effect at the youngest age possible. We thereby give them the means to create well-being in their lives.

What Should Parents Give Their Kids?

Protection through containment. And what is containment? Rules.

> *Rules are a protective, respectful, and nurturing fence that we place around our children for their well-being.*

We know what is best for our children because we are older and more experienced. Think of yourself as the good shepherd and your child or children as your flock. Keep them in the sheepfold under watchful eye and protection. If they try to leave the containment, they may put themselves in danger. A good shepherd would never knowingly put his charges in harm's way. The fences of the fold are the rules that you and your mate have established. These rules are the result of how seriously you take your role as a guardian, protector, guide, and mentor. When a sheep wishes to go outside the fold, it must be restrained for its own good.

From the sheep's point of view, you are inhibiting its right to free expression. Be assured that even if the fences or rules you use are fair and equitable, your child will see them as punishment. No matter, for you want to be a good shepherd. Whether or not your flock loves you is not the issue. "Job one" is to protect and nourish them.

When children break the rules, they must understand the consequences of their negative action. They will perceive it as *punishment*. You see it as containment: keeping them safe.

It is important to note that your response to their negative action must always be a cause and not an effect. *Never react in anger.*

Be firm and fair with your rules, and be consistent. Children can't be expected to follow your rules if they are not sure what the rules are from day to day. Your children also need to know that consequences for negative behaviour will always and absolutely follow. No excuses. No exceptions.

Keep in mind that the foundation of all these rules must contain an essential component of the Perfect System. Yes, by now you must know what we are going to say!

> **CAUSE AND EFFECT:** *For every action there is an equal and opposite reaction.*

In the physical world this law never varies. It is indisputable. Learn it and teach it to your children.

- Negative actions beget negative reactions.
- Positive actions beget positive reactions.

Therefore we are responsible for virtually everything that happens to us.

What Should We Nurture in Our Kids?

Let's close this chapter by discussing the concept of "prodigious qualities."

A prodigious quality is a genius that each of us is born with. Most of the time it goes unrecognized, but it is our job as parents to find and nurture this quality in each of our children.

The value attached to these qualities changes with every culture and generation. Back in the Hellenistic era, clear thinking and social skills were considered attractive and valued. Therefore these skills were promoted when discovered. The "special" children who showed them were nurtured and so was their prodigious skill. In our culture, computer skills and musical skills are highly valued.

> *A child's prodigious quality is a direct channel to his or her personal fulfillment.*

When your child's prodigious quality is recognized and supported, you will have given your child the greatest gift. Why? Because this recognition and support will lead to that child's fulfillment.

It is the shortest path to actualizing your child's human potential. Think of it this way: We are all musicians in life's orchestra. Each of us has an instrument to play — a task to perform — that is unique and individual. When we recognize our children's prodigious quality, we are allowing them to play the instrument they were born to play. Imagine the frustration of being a gifted musician and not being able to play your instrument of choice, or worse, not being allowed to play at all.

Prodigious attributes must first be recognized, and then promoted and taught. A seven-year-old genius violinist didn't become this extraordinary performer overnight. Excellence doesn't just happen. It needs focus and mentoring. The prodigious quality was identified, proper education was given, and only then could that quality be maximized.

Always remember the truth we discussed in earlier chapters: Your child is not a clone of you. Parents who have been lucky enough to discover and exercise their own prodigious quality often seek to identify and force-feed this same quality in their children. Others push qualities or ambitions that they wish they had been able to pursue themselves. This is a big mistake. What happens when children are pushed to display a talent they may not possess or that they possess to a lesser degree than the parent or that they're just plain not interested in? They end up feeling resentful toward the parent and anxious about their own failure to live up to expectations. Worse, these children's genuine prodigious qualities may go undiscovered and un-nurtured. They may never discover complete fulfillment.

Some of you may be saying: "I don't think my child has a prodigious quality. He has shown no special talent in any area. If I pretend to see a talent in some direction — maybe something I'm interested in — and if I provide lots of praise and support, won't this encourage my child to improve and find success?"

Absolutely not, because your child is going to figure out that your praise is inherently false. And more importantly, because you will not be nurturing the genuine prodigious quality your child was born with.

There is a vast list of qualities that we often don't look for in our children: social skills, practical aptitude, natural generosity, superior verbal skills, and all kinds of other valuable things.

> It is our duty to look beyond the obvious to discover our child's prodigious quality.

Try to expose your children to a broad range of social, intellectual, cultural, and physical opportunities to help uncover their special interests and talents. When the prodigious quality begins to make itself visible — and it will if you look hard enough — provide the guidance, support, and nurturing that will allow it to reach its full glorious potential.

4

The Rules of Parenting

Constancy and consistency are two key components of success in parenting. Changing the rules mid-game is not fair and is confusing. Inconsistency is actually dangerous for a child: the mixed messages that it sends leave them confused and unsure of their place in their small universe. Give your child a fighting chance to win the game.

Consistency in the home gives children security. They are confronted with more than enough changes in their outside world. Technology is constantly changing, which changes society in both obvious and subtle ways. Your kids are bombarded with changing messages from all sides. But whatever you may sometimes think, you remain the most important influencer in your child's world. You are your child's example. You are your child's prime teacher. Be consistent. Practice zero tolerance. Take your responsibilities as a teacher seriously.

How Children Learn

Your actions are subliminally teaching your children how to behave. Language does not have the impact on children that we think. The way we speak and act are far more influential. We call this "ambience." We will discuss this more fully when we get into the "ages and stages" chapters of this book.

Another truth is that we are the products of our parents — just as they were the products of their parents, ad infinitum. In many respects, though it is difficult for most of us to acknowledge, we are the same parents our parents were to us. There have been all kinds of research into alcoholic fathers breeding alcoholic sons and divorced homes begetting divorced homes. Why does this phenomenon occur?

To answer this I (Syd) would like to tell you about a lesson one of my close female friends taught me. It was the beginning of a fresh understanding for me as a new parent.

This woman had a boyfriend whose father was a professional wrestler. As her boyfriend was growing up, his father would greet him every time he came home by putting him in a headlock and rubbing his knuckles against his head. I believe this is called a "noogie." It was just his way of saying that he loved his son.

Eventually the son left home to go to college. He met a beautiful woman and the two of them started to live together. The problem was that the first time he came home after moving in with her, he put her in a headlock and give her a noogie.

"What the hell are you doing?" she said.

"I am showing you how much I love you," he said, surprised.

The noogie was the only way he knew to express physical love when greeting someone precious to him. He told her the story of how he had been raised by his father. She then informed him that there were other ways to show affection, ways that she had learned from her parents, like hugging and kissing and speaking softly.

> *As children, we learned from our parents' actions how to love, communicate, react, and behave.*

It is possible to break this generational cycle, but it takes a lot of honesty and desire to change. It takes patience, sensitivity, and non-judgment from the important people around us. As we have said, it also takes consistent rules.

Rules to Parent By

Here are the rules you can apply to your children for their greatest benefit.

Rule #1

Parent with consistency

Nothing creates more confusion in a child's experience than inconsistency.

> *Inconsistency undermines the rules of Cause and Effect laid down by the parent(s). Conversely, consistency reinforces and accelerates the child's understanding of these rules.*

When you behave inconsistently as a parent and your child is at a cognitive stage to realize this, it is vital for you to acknowledge the breach and then apologize for the inconsistency. Using words like "I wasn't thinking when I ..." or "I did a bad action when I ..." reflects to the child that making mistakes is not the end of the world as long as they acknowledge them and apologize for them. When you do this as a parent, you are showing respect for the child and for the rule that was broken. By apologizing, you also allow your child to see you as not perfect but human — as someone facing the same kinds of challenges they do.

Rule #2

Never fall prey to the "divide and conquer" strategem
Father and mother are one unit. This unity creates deep security for a child.

If there are two parents in the home, the parents should always act with one mind and voice. There should be one opinion and one rule. A child should never be allowed to drive a wedge between the parents, and their unity must never be broken in the eyes of a child. Mother and Father are one.

With this in mind, we spent lots of time creating our parenting rule book, and made a pact that we would never let our kids come between us and make us pawns in their control game.

First we co-created the rule book and agreed that we would follow the same rules together, all the time, no matter what. That meant that when one of our kids got us alone, we would never let them influence us to go against the other parent's ruling. Our response, when children said things like, "But Mommy said I could ...," was to ask the child exactly what the other parent had said about the matter, and to check that with our mate.

We never went against each other's individual rulings *even if one of us thought the other was wrong*. To our mind, there was no percentage in not backing the other parent. The lesson was about unity, not separation. In this way the children got a double whammy, accelerating their learning process.

Rule #3

You, and not your child, are at the top of the family hierarchy
Make it clear to your children that your mate is more important to you than they are. Your mate comes first; then they do. This is a difficult notion for parents to get their heads around. However, it teaches children the importance of parental unity. It also teaches them that the family does not revolve around them and their needs.

To reiterate, there is a caveat to the above statement. Unity must be modelled even in a divorced situation. The family unit is just that: a unit. We acknowledge that this book is written from the mindset that there are two parents under one roof. However, the principles in this book apply even when parents are separated. It just takes cooperation and the desire, from both parties, to raise emotionally healthy children.

There are some situations that we have not specifically addressed: for example, an uncooperative or absent mate. If you are forced to be a single parent, the rules in our book still hold true. It will just take a little more ingenuity and patience.

Not only do we as a society neglect to teach children the critical concept of Cause and Effect, we also fail to bring up our children with realistic expectations of their place and role versus others. This begins with a failure to give children a correct understanding of the family pecking order and their place within it.

As a parent, it is your responsibility to manage your children's expectations by teaching them that parents, not the child, come first in that pecking order.

For example, you should teach your child never to interrupt when you and your mate are talking. (One side note: Rules are not written in granite. In an emergency, of course your child should interrupt.) If you don't do this, if you put the child first in the household, you are establishing an unrealistic model that will create unrealistic expectations as your child moves into adulthood. Not to speak of lots of chaos along the way.

If the children are *first*, then someone else is *second*. This concept is contrary to the Perfect System, which is about service to others, about caring for others before ourselves. The Perfect System guarantees the outcome of most events and relationships in our lives because, at the end of the day, we get back out of life exactly what we put into it. Our behaviour determines our outcomes.

> *Young children must be shown through ambience and eventually discussion that Mommy and Daddy's needs come first, not theirs.*

Most kids grow up to have false expectations about how they should be treated and what they are worthy of. This is the basis of their feelings of entitlement. We can avoid this by introducing our children to the concept of hierarchy in the house as soon as they begin to gain cognitive and verbal understanding — in other words, between 1 1/2 and 3 years of age.

We decided that we were not going to devalue our close relationship just because we had kids. This may sound selfish, but it is a very important concept. It created great unity and genuine love between us as adults. It taught our kids that they had a place in our home and lives but did not own or control that place. This was a form of containment, bringing a sense of great security to our children.

Rule #4

Everything has a consequence

We have already discussed the importance of rules. They provide a child with protection and security. However, before a rule is broken, you must put in place a mechanism for the child to discuss mitigating circumstances. Fairness and flexibility, case by case, are essential.

But what happens when children break the rules without mitigating circumstances, going outside the sheepfold we have built for their benefit?

It is difficult to contain our children consistently. Why? We always want them to love us. We are terrified of losing their affection. However, the paradox is that the more contained our kids are, the more they will love and appreciate us.

When children break the rules, they must understand the consequences of their negative actions. Breaking rules must always be followed by containment, which they will see as punishment. The consequence we always used was loss of community privilege.

> *Being alone is the worst consequence for a child.*

People who don't behave in an acceptable manner are removed from society until they can understand the rules of that society. The same is true in families. Being alone is even more painful for a child than a harsh look, a cross word, or a spanking.

Spanking has no place in good parenting. When you spank a child, the child controls you because you are in a reactive state. What have you really taught the child? You have only validated the idea that overpowering someone smaller and weaker is appropriate behaviour. A haunting cartoon on this point ran in *The New Yorker* thirty years ago. It showed a mother spanking a toddler held over her knee. The mother's caption read, "This'll teach you not to hit someone smaller than you!" This is obviously not a good lesson to teach a child. What children need and crave is acceptance from the parent. They want to feel fulfilled, and the parents are the child's prime source of fulfillment. Our children are nourished by our approval and acknowledgment.

> When you discipline a child, never do it in anger.

If you get angry, it signals that a behaviour on the child's part can trigger an emotion in you. This is a negative lesson because you want to be the cause, not the effect. Always respond with respect. Remember, when you punish, you are teaching a lesson. As a teacher, you can never take the matter personally. It is a job that needs clear thinking — decision-making that is not muddled by negative emotions.

Rule #5

When a child misbehaves, always give the child three choices
Here are the choices we gave:

Choice #1: Stop the inappropriate action.
Choice #2: If you do not stop, then please leave my presence and go to your room. You may come out when you can live by the rules established in the house.
Choice #3: If you will not go to your room by yourself, then I will take you by the hand to your room.

Let's look at the positive aspects of each choice.

- Choice #1 gives the child the ability to take control of her behaviour in a positive, proactive manner. You are teaching your child to take responsibility for her actions. This understanding will prove to be a priceless legacy and will ultimately become her tool for success as she becomes an adult.
- Choice #2 allows the child to keep face. She is still misbehaving, but the choice still puts the outcome and responsibility in her hands.
- Choice #3 is a humiliating experience for a child because she has lost total control of the situation. The child has been contained in a non-harmful manner — at the end of the experience she is still allowed to come out and join the rest of the family, as long as she agrees to follow the rules and be part of the greater community.

Always give choices, because the ability to create choices will serve your children well in adulthood. The more choices they have, the more possibilities they will experience and the better able they will be to choose beneficial outcomes.

As we will discuss in more detail in the chapters on ages and stages, children should be exposed to increasing choices as they grow older. This must in no way negate the existence or importance of rules and consequences. Just as with young children, permanent house rules must remain, along with additional age-appropriate specific rules. As parents, however, we may choose to invite input from an older child into the appropriate consequence for breaking a rule. Some parents of older children write the house rules down in a contract that includes agreed-upon consequences for good and bad behaviour.

Rule #6

Make sure the rules, the reason for the rules, and the consequences for breaking the rules are clear and understood.
In order to comply, your children need to know what behaviour and actions are expected of them. They also need to know what is not acceptable to you as parents. Rules are how you make this clear. They tell your children where the fences are.

Some family rules are so important, and so much a part of your value system, that they have to be considered permanent. These would include rules about kind and considerate behaviour. Start talking about these rules from your child's earliest age. Say things like, "In this house, we try not to fight." And "In this family, we try to help each other."

> *Say the rules often; live them all the time.*

As parents, we also need to develop specific rules as time goes by to fit different ages, family needs, and, in many cases, changing behaviours. In these instances, it is our responsibility as parents to sit down with our children and spell out what the new rules are, why they are being introduced, and what the penalties will be if the new rules are broken.

Never come up with new rules in the heat of the moment, when you and your child are feeling emotional. You are the teacher. Think carefully and clearly about your parental responsibility to your child, consciously consider what rules will be best for your child's welfare, and then communicate your decision to the child in an objective, reasoned manner. Choose calm and unemotional periods for these important conversations.

Let's say your young child starts throwing tantrums every evening before bed when told to tidy her toys. You might choose to bring up the topic at a relaxed moment in the morning before the toys come out. You might say: "We know you don't like to put all your toys away at night, but we can't accept the room being left in a mess, and we can't accept you screaming when we tell you to tidy up. So we are going to have a new rule: from now on, starting right now, the rule is that you can have only one toy out in the room at a time. If you have one toy out and you decide you want to play with something else, you must put the other toy away first. Only one toy at a time — that's the new rule. It means you won't have lots of toys to tidy away before bedtime, so we will all be much happier. Do you understand the rule?"

We wanted to teach our children that as a family we are all responsible for each other's welfare. So in our house we didn't care which kid started the fight. When there was a fight, both got punished. We wanted to teach them that, in our house, blame was a currency with no value. We also wanted them to learn how to solve their personal issues between themselves in a kind and sharing manner. They understood from our position that they rose and fell together. They learned how to diffuse potentially negative situations. They began to understand that there was nothing in it for them if they squealed on each other. The result was having two kids who eventually never argued aggressively and who became each other's protector. Just as important, we created a peaceful household filled with discussion, not debate, a house where division was frowned upon and sharing rewarded.

If you have an older child and decide to spell out the house rules and consequences in a contract, remember that such contracts need to be reviewed regularly to ensure that the rules remain appropriate to the child's age and/or the family's needs.

> *If a rule becomes age-inappropriate or unnecessary, don't just let the rule slide.*

Letting a rule just fade away without discussion will give the impression that rules aren't important and can be tossed out or ignored willy-nilly. Instead, have a conversation to discuss how the rule is no longer needed and is therefore no longer in effect. Talk about why.

The Power of Ambience

In closing, we would like to illustrate the point stated at the beginning of this chapter: that our actions are the most influential forces in our children's moral and conscious growth. Never underestimate the power of this ambience. We heard a great illustration of this point from one of our teachers, Karen Berg.

Once there was a man who was very old and went to live with his son. But the son couldn't find room for the father in the house, so he gave his father a blanket and sent him to sleep in the barn.

It became very cold and started to rain heavily. Still the father remained in the barn. That night the son went to say goodnight to his father and saw that the blanket had been cut in half, leaving his father with only half a blanket.

"Who did this to the blanket?" the son asked.

"Your son did this," the father replied.

"My son did such a terrible thing? How could he do such a horrible thing?" With anger in his heart he ran out of the barn, into the house, up the stairs, and into his son's room.

"How could you do this? Why did you cut your grandfather's blanket in two?" he asked his son. Then he saw the other half of the blanket next to his son's bed. "And why did you take the other half of the blanket?"

"Because I am saving it for you, Father."

Part 3

The System Through the Ages and Stages

5

Up to Age 3

No other stage in life holds as many changes in every area — physical, cognitive, and social — as the first few years. And we as parents have been given the exquisite responsibility of nurturing, protecting, guiding, and overseeing our children through every single step of this critical period. These are the years that will form the foundation of the rest of their lives.

Are you a new parent? We know well the anxiety you may be feeling at the start of this important journey. It seems a monumental task — because that's exactly what parenting is. But know that if you follow the principles of the Perfect System of Parenting, you and your child are at the start of a most fascinating voyage, one that will ultimately prove full of joy and fulfillment. Most importantly, it will result in a wonderful, loving, happy child — and eventually, an amazing man or woman.

Newborn

During the first few weeks, your baby is learning to adjust to a completely new life outside the womb. Your newborn's behaviour is a reaction to the lack of the female world around them. As a parent you are similarly adjusting to a completely new world in the womb of your new family. Your life may feel as if it has been turned inside out. Every day may feel like chaos.

This is not surprising. Your baby is still adjusting to independent life, which means physical development and behavioural patterns are completely haphazard, making it difficult for you to feel in control. In fact, as you run around reacting to your baby's demands every moment of the day and night, you may even start to feel the frustration of being the domino at the end of the row.

The question is: As parents of newborns, is it ever possible to be a cause rather than an effect?

The answer is, yes, absolutely! Start by accepting that your newborn's unpredictable, changing needs must totally dictate the way your days physically unfold for a while. Know that this will not last for long. Accept it as one hundred percent normal and as a necessary and positive part of the parent-child relationship that you are beginning to forge.

Nurturing above all

You are your child's nurturer, and during the very first few weeks this is your only role. If you dedicate yourself to this first task of providing totally and utterly for your newborn's needs, you will begin to feel genuine peace and satisfaction.

> *In putting another person's needs completely ahead of your own, you are, like the First Cause, giving all.*

As we've discussed in previous chapters, this is the route to true fulfillment. What a wonderful way to begin the parent-child relationship! It also ensures that you become the cause and not the effect.

Learning through ambience

Remember that even at this early age, your baby picks up on your moods. As we discussed in chapter 4, our actions as parents are subliminally teaching our children on an ongoing basis. We call this ambience. The way you speak and act will ultimately have far more impact on your child than the actual words you use. Newborns soak up ambience, reacting to the way we act and the tone of our speech.

We began our process immediately after our first son, Jacob, was born. We realized that even though he was not yet cognitive, he was still picking up on our ambience. That was defined by the physical body language we used when responding to his crying, the look on our faces, the tone of our voices, the intent of our touch. All of these signalled our desire for his sense of fulfillment.

We recognized that his desire for fulfillment was infantile. His own fulfillment was his only desire. He wasn't thinking, at 3 a.m. in the morning, "I think I'll not cry now — Mommy needs a good night's sleep." But we put no limitation or judgment on his needs because that was the world he understood and was dealing with at that moment. However, he could feel that we cared more about him than we did about ourselves. We were imprinting him the only way possible.

> The first law of the Perfect System is taught non-verbally through our physical actions.

We knew that our son's behaviour would not change at that moment. But the behavioural foundation was laid on which both parent and child would later build when he became aware of abstract ideas.

The Newborn Stage: Key Messages Recapped

- In the first few weeks, your key role is to be your child's nurturer. In putting his or her needs ahead of your own, you are giving all. This is the route to true fulfillment.
- Your baby is learning through ambience. Let your actions show your baby that you care about his or her fulfillment more than anything else, and that you are giving all.
The first law of the Perfect System is being taught non-verbally.

The Baby Months

At around two months, your baby will suddenly surprise you with that wonderful first smile. Your helpless, passive newborn is becoming an individual little being, able to interact and show pleasure and displeasure. In the next few weeks, you'll be treated to cooing and gurgling. And at about three months, your tiny child will laugh out loud. You will become convinced that for whatever reason, you and your mate have been chosen to parent the most adorable little being the world has ever seen!

Interaction with others

The closer you get to six months, the more your baby will interact with you, and the more interest your baby will show in the surrounding world. Remember the importance of teaching through ambience. Your child learns from soaking up the actions of others. Respond to this natural curiosity by propping baby up when awake, helping him or her observe what is going on and learn from you and other adults.

By the time they reach seven to nine months, babies start demonstrating an increasingly complex range of emotions — everything from frustration, anger, and resentment to shyness and anxiety. Be very careful to model the positive emotions that you hope your child will display in future years. Avoid being around your baby when you feel bad-tempered or frustrated — and never ever respond to your baby's behaviour with a show of anger. If you feel your emotions brimming up, put your baby safely in someone else's hands or in its crib, and go to your bedroom and count to ten. Take a deep breath and calm down before you return to your baby's side.

Constantly show that you are thoughtful and caring of baby's needs and emotions. As babies get older, for example, many become anxious about being separated from Mommy or Daddy and may cry when held by other adults. Let baby get comfortable and familiar with visitors before being held by them. Demonstrate that you are your child's protector.

> *Show that your child's need for fulfillment is of paramount importance to you.*

Cause and Effect

Seven to nine months is also a time when you can introduce the essential concept of Cause and Effect. "Introduce" is probably not the best word, of course, since babies become acquainted with the concept the first time they realize that when they cry, Mommy comes, and that when they smile or coo or gurgle, every adult within reach makes a huge fuss over them.

Once you head toward the last quarter of your baby's first year, however, prepare to see the baby trying out more advanced Cause and Effect techniques. You're probably familiar with one example: the baby is in a high chair or stroller, and supposedly drops a toy. What does the nearest parent do? Why, pick it up and hand it back to the baby, of course! Now what does the baby do? She promptly drops it back over the side, leans over to stare at it, and then turns expectantly to the parent. The parent picks it up and hands it back. Baby grins and repeats the process — ad infinitum, if you allow it.

What has happened here? Baby has you running. Your tiny child is in control and loves the feeling. Your baby is just exploring — but power over others is a heady experience.

This is an excellent opportunity to begin teaching the lesson that every action has a consequence — and that sometimes the consequence is not getting what you want. Let's look at a way to handle the situation that will jump-start this message.

1. The first time your baby drops the toy, pick it up and hand it back, saying something like: "Keep this on your tray. If it's on the floor, you won't have a toy to play with." Your baby may not understand the words but will gradually learn to pick up on the tone.
2. When the baby immediately drops the toy back over the side, leave it on the floor, saying something like: "Now you don't have a toy to play with."
3. Tears are likely at this point. Distract your baby with another activity. The objective isn't an unhappy child but introducing the principle that will serve your child well throughout life: Every action has an equal and opposite reaction. Negative actions beget negative reactions. Positive actions beget positive reactions. Or, from your baby's point of view, "When I don't throw my toy on the floor, I still have a toy to play with."

The Baby Months: Key Messages Recapped

- This is a time for consistent teaching through ambience. As your baby develops a more complex range of emotions, be careful to model positive emotions and avoid negative emotions. Never show anger when around your baby.
- Continue to demonstrate that your baby's need for true fulfillment is your priority.
- In the simplest possible ways, begin to introduce the concept of Cause and Effect: negative actions beget negative reactions; positive actions beget positive reactions.

Ages 1 ½ to 3

Batten down the hatches. Here come the "terrible twos." Terrible for toddlers and terrible for you. And don't be misled by the term: This trying period can start several months prior to age 2 and go on for several months into age 3. Sorry!

The time spent with your child now becomes increasingly more intense. He, with all the skill of a Russian chess champion, will become a genius at manipulating others for the fulfillment of his needs. This is major shift time. Your personal life will become secondary to this tornado of activity and growth. It is a most trying time, because what was once cute and cuddly has become cantankerous and insensitive. That sucking sound you hear is your child's vacuum of wants and needs.

Many books have been written about this time in a child's growth, so we will leave it to the experts to describe the "why" of this potentially calamitous time. But the bottom line is your son or daughter is now becoming a cognitive thinker.

> *This is a pivotal time to convert ambient teaching to a more cerebral, verbal understanding.*

Teaching through words

For us, it was a time to show that we also existed in our son's world; that we also had needs. It was Jacob's opportunity to start to explore the possibility of sharing. We had a window of opportunity to create a behaviour contract between child and parents.

We thought long and hard about this manifesto of rights and expectations. After much rehearsal, we waited for the right opportunity and then struck like lightning. At a point when he was getting more and more out of control, we sat down and had a conversation with him, the gist of which was this:

> We are not happy with the way you are acting. Because you are so young you may not know when you are acting badly, so Mommy and Daddy will give you a signal to stop that bad behaviour. If we are alone, we will tell you to stop. If you don't stop, then we will start to count to three, like this: 'One, two, three.' If you are with other people, we will get your attention with a hand signal and with our fingers we will count silently: 'one, two, three.' If you do not stop misbehaving, you will then have two choices. The first choice is to go to your room and stay there until you are ready to come out and be with us. If you don't go by yourself, the second choice is that either Mommy or Daddy will take you by the hand to your room. And of course you can come out again after you decide you want to be with us and our rules.

We told him that we loved him very much and it was important to us that he listen when we said "stop." "Your misbehaving may put you in danger," we said, "like touching something you shouldn't or going someplace you shouldn't. You are a little boy and we are your parents, and we know what is best for you."

This was our speech, and an example of the tone and linear thinking we had both agreed on. You may choose different words. Nevertheless, following are the key concepts involved.

- Parents are the boss, because safety issues come first.
- A child may have some independence as he or she begins to explore.
- There is such a thing as a child's time and your time, a child's needs and your needs.
- There are rules of acceptable behaviour.
- A child has choices to make about how to act, and these choices will have an impact on whether the child feels happy or sad.

After our talk, we let him get away with a few instances of improper behaviour. We wanted the right opportunity to reinforce the key concepts — that moment when he was misbehaving just to get a rise out of us.

We didn't have to wait long. One day he was acting crazy. The key word is "acting." When the moment was right, we struck like a blitzkrieg and asked him to stop his misbehaving. He did. We applauded his behaviour. This happened three or four times in a row. Of course we were really impressed with our superior intelligence — until one dark and dingy day when he took it up a notch and went berserk in front of our astonished eyes. This was one of those unstoppable berserks that called for an elephant tranquilizer. So we were forced to go to "code red." We had to revert to the *three count* — culminating in taking him by the hand to his bedroom. Of course this is an understatement, because the moment I (Syd), grabbed his hand, he went limp. I was forced to carry him à la Frank Buck ("Bring 'em back alive") kicking and screaming to his room. Our son had transformed himself into an uncontrollable wild thing.

> *This is why you want to start your behaviour training at a young age!*

If you need to get tough, it is best to do so when your child is two or three years old. When children get bigger, it is harder to manifest a three count. But it must be done to validate to your child that you mean what you say and you say what you mean.

At this point we must re-emphasize that you must never punish your child in anger. You must always be calm in your demeanour.

> *If you get angry, it signals to children that their behaviour can trigger an emotion in you.*

This is a bad lesson because you want to be the cause, not the effect. Being unemotional tells your child it is not personal. It is just you keeping your word, as you stated in your practiced speech.

Jacob cried himself to sleep. We consistently visited him in his room and reminded him that he could come out whenever he chose to behave in the appropriate manner. It seemed like an eternity to Ellen and me. It was just as painful for us as it was for him, but we knew the point had to be made. It was a control and role issue.

Teach your child to listen

This is a good time to stress the importance of active listening. You want your child to listen to what you have to say, so it's important to model active listening when your child speaks. When your children are talking, look them in the eyes to show that you value what they have to say. Get down to their level, lean forward a little, and echo back some of the words they have used, to prove you are listening and to ensure that there's no miscommunication. For example, after your child has pleaded to go to the park, you might say: "I hear what you're saying. You would really like to go to the park to play on the swings. I can see you would really like to do that. At the moment, Mommy and I are busy, but we will go to the park to play on the swings after we've all had lunch. Would you like that?"

Reinforce parental unity

Remember the vital importance of parental unity that we discussed in the last chapter. Mother and Father are one, and will never go against each other. Consistent unity provides your child with security. It also limits your child's ability to manipulate the family.

Establish hierarchy in the house

An important lesson follows naturally from the understanding of parents as one unit. Now is the time to firmly communicate to your child the previously discussed critical message: Mommy and Daddy's needs come first. He is not the most important focus in the home. This model also works when siblings enter the scene. They must fit into the family — not control it.

We consistently stood by this. We didn't jump just because our kids wanted something. We finished what we were doing. It was simple. We just said something like, "I will help you after I finish what I'm doing."

We were not harsh about it, just matter of fact. It was not a steadfast rule, but we applied it whenever we could, teaching our kids the notion that they were not the most important people in our house. They learned from Daddy that Mommy came before them in the hierarchy chain, and they learned from Mommy that Daddy was ahead of them. It was a great technique for defusing any spoiled behaviour.

Teach appropriate ways to talk

The secret here is whispering. This is a stroke of genius for parents who want their kids to experience it all — which should, of course, be *every* parent.

We were older parents and really wanted our children to experience as much of life as possible — and to experience it alongside us. So at the earliest possible age, we taught our kids the **magic key** to enjoying music, museums, plays, and movies, going to adults' houses, and so on.

> We taught them how to WHISPER.

It is so simple and effective, yet so many parents never teach their kids that there is a time to speak in a soft voice and a time to speak in a regular voice. By giving our children the magic power of whispering, we made it possible for us to take them regularly to concerts before they were three years old. When they wanted to ask a question or needed to go to the bathroom, they knew that the proper behaviour was to whisper into our ears.

The lesson was twofold. Here's what they learned:

1. With the proper behaviour, we can have the most wonderful experiences together.

2. It is important for us to consider other people's feelings. Disturbing people is not acceptable behaviour.

As a result, our children became knowledgeable about the arts, culture, and social issues way beyond their years. To this day they have a "reference catalogue" equivalent to that of a 50-year-old.

> **Ages 1 ½ to 3: Key Messages Recapped**
> - Begin to move from ambient teaching to more cerebral, verbal communication. Communicate that there are rules of acceptable behaviour. Teach that the parent is the boss because safety comes first.
> - Be consistent in your own behaviour toward your child, and show a consistent, solidly-united front with your partner. Establish appropriate hierarchy in the house.
> - When your child misbehaves, always give choices.
> - Teach your child to listen — and teach appropriate voices for speaking.
> - Imprint the notion of putting another person's needs before one's own by introducing "sharing" concepts such as "your time" and "our time," "your needs" and "our needs."
> - Teach and demonstrate that your child has choices of actions that will have an impact on whether he or she feels happy or sad. Positive actions beget positive reactions; negative actions beget negative reactions. This is a critical early lesson on the principle of Cause and Effect. We all need lasting fulfillment, and an understanding of Cause and Effect will allow us to meet this need.

6

From 3 to 5

From toddler to child. It's a big leap forward and one that fills children with a sense of self as they become emotionally and physically more self-sufficient: "I can do things by myself now! Look out, world — here I come!"

Reinforce Containment

The challenge for parents at this stage is to foster in their children a positive and accurate self-image and encourage independent exploration, all within the sheepfold that we have erected for their safety and for family happiness. Make sure that rules of containment are firmly in place to protect your child and maintain appropriate behaviour while still allowing them the freedom to develop cognitively, socially, and physically.

If it sounds difficult, remember that you have one big thing in your favour: your child is developing impressive new verbal abilities, together with increasing memory.

> *By age 5, most children can use over 2,000 words and probably understand up to 13,000.*

This makes it infinitely easier for you to communicate and enforce house rules — and to begin explaining the "why" behind them.

When a child misbehaves, remember to always give the child three choices:

Choice #1: Stop the inappropriate action.
Choice #2: If you do not stop, then please leave my presence and go to your room. You may come out when you can live by the behavioural rules established in the house.
Choice #3: If you will not go to your room by yourself, then I will take you by the hand to your room.

Imprint Cause and Effect

Take advantage of the fact that children of this age develop an acute awareness of the concept of rules. Just keep in mind that everything is black and white for them — they are not subtle in their interpretation. This is a great opportunity to further imprint the notion of Cause and Effect. It makes good sense to children at this stage of their development.

- I do good things = good things happen.
- I do things that are not so good = not so good things happen.

Constantly reinforce this concept. Make sure your child's good behaviour is always rewarded with a heaping dose of attention, or even with physical rewards such as stickers or other treats. In the same way, bad behaviour must always receive a consequence.

> *Keep demonstrating the link between Cause and Effect. It won't be long before your child grasps the simple logic of this critical principle.*

Verbally Introduce the Concept of Empathy

Along with a new awareness of rules, your little child is discovering a moral sense: a sense of right and wrong and of fairness. This may go along with a new sensitivity to other people's feelings. This is something you can foster.

During these years your child is developing relationships with other children and adults in the wider universe. Build empathy by talking about how your child feels when others act in certain ways. Talk about how your child's actions have the same effect on others. When your child does something unkind, it makes another child feel bad, and the result is that the other child is unkind back. The domino effect.

Seize this opportunity to introduce the importance of doing kind acts for other people. Emphasize the good feelings that your child will experience as a result. By doing this, you will be introducing the concept of fulfillment, along with its relationship to Cause and Effect.

> *Role playing is a valuable tool for getting some of these concepts across.*

Children of this age love to play-act. They play at being Mommy or Daddy and can easily be encouraged to extend their role playing to other characters in their universe. It's a great way to help children almost literally put themselves in the shoes of others.

Critical Lessons Through Containment

We're afraid you'll find, around this time, that your child's new sense of right and wrong and fairness will also likely lead to the development of squabbles with siblings and friends. Children of this age will loudly — even forcefully — defend what they believe are their own rights and entitlements and the "rules of the game."

A year and a half after the birth of Jacob, we had Isaac, our second child. He was a sponge. He not only picked up our ambience but was feeding off his brother's as well. We believe this was a contributing factor to his accelerated learning. Jacob was his Missouri ("as Missouri goes, so goes the Nation"). We had survived Jacob's "terrible twos." The lessons were in the air and Isaac synergistically understood the rules of the game. When Jacob was $4\,1/2$, Isaac was 3. They loved to play video games together. Then the arguments started: "I killed you ... you've got to stay dead!" You know the drill.

Again this was simply another teaching opportunity for us as parents. "This is not appropriate behaviour in our house," we said. "You are not allowed to act in this manner. We are a sharing family, and this unsharing way of acting is not acceptable."

Of course one of the boys piped up with, "It wasn't my fault. He started it!"

Aha, another opportunity! "Fault doesn't count in this house," we said, "because we all need to be thinking about protecting and caring for each other. Blame means that someone is not doing their protecting job. So next time we hear any arguments when you guys are playing video games, here's what happens. There is no three-count. The machine will immediately be turned off and you will not be allowed to play again for that day. You can go read a book or play catch, but no video games."

The next day, again at the video game, we heard whispers coming from the room where they were playing.

"That's not fair, you were dead and now you're alive," Isaac was saying in a very low voice,

"If Mom and Dad hear us, we will not be able to play," Jacob shot back, also *sotto voce*.

Isaac thought for a second and said, "OK, let's start the game over."

It was an amazing moment for us. Because we had been thoughtful in containing their behaviour, they were able to solve a potentially volatile situation of their own volition. They had a great learning experience. And they controlled it. They took the responsibility for the outcome of their event and converted two I's to We. They were starting to understand collective responsibility — the power of unity and the power of Cause and Effect.

The Importance of Multi-sensory Experiences

Physically, cognitively, and socially, children develop in leaps and bounds between the ages of 3 and 5. They achieve mature gross motor control, which gives them a whole pile of physical play options, from skipping, jumping, hopping, balancing, and running to riding a bicycle and playing ball. Their rapidly-developing fine-motor skills also mean they enjoy arts and crafts and copying Mommy and Daddy in grooming tasks. And, not to be overlooked, full-scale cognitive advances result in a love of colours, fantasy games, rhymes and songs, and other creative play.

Give them every opportunity to explore *all* of these important development areas. For you and them to ultimately discover and develop their prodigious quality, they need to be exposed to as many options and skill areas as possible. They are little sponges at this stage.

When you are taking your children out, remember to reinforce the magic power of whispering that you introduced when they first achieved cognitive and verbal understanding. Their knowledge of the importance of using appropriate voices for different occasions will allow you to introduce them to a wonderfully wide world of experiences.

We used the same three-count rule when we were out with our two kids. If they did not whisper, we gave them the choices. We meant what we said and said what we meant. We had to take them home from an event once. They knew our rules were not breakable. As always, consistency had to be maintained, and although it annoyed us to leave the theatre on that occasion, we felt that our job as teachers and mentors was more important than any single entertainment event. It never happened again.

So use the magic tool of whispering to take your child with you to museums and art galleries. Attend young-theatre performances and kids' concerts. Go to concerts in the park. Go to restaurants together. Visit adult friends' homes. Go to professional ball games and neigbourhood games.

At home or on fun trips out, play in the water together. Hike and explore the countryside. Create your own nature adventures in your backyard or local park. Finger paint or throw paint on canvas. Use modelling clay to make your own characters and animals, and then use them as performers in your own made-up plays. Read together. Count together. Sing and dance together. Play together. Have fun together! You will be teaching your child some of the most important lessons in life.

Ages 3 to 5: Key Messages Recapped

- Teach through containment. Be one hundred percent consistent.
- Always give misbehaving children the three choices.
- Take advantage of your child's increasing verbal and cognitive skills to discuss rules and the reasons behind them.
- Reinforce concepts taught earlier, such as family hierarchy and the unity of parents.
- Verbally introduce the concept of empathy, relating it to the concept of fulfillment.
- Imprint the critical Cause and Effect principle.
- Take advantage of role playing to explain concepts.
- Expose your child to multi-sensory experiences.

7

From 6 to 9

Between 6 and 9 years, children go through a period of enormous intellectual growth. They learn to read and write and count and multiply. They also develop a longer attention span and a much more sophisticated cognitive understanding that allows them to start grasping truly abstract concepts.

Keep in mind that, both physically and cognitively, there are major variances in children's development over these years. Some kids are early starters, while others take their time and save themselves for a winning sprint at the end. About the only thing we can say for certain is that there will be surprises and challenges as children begin to develop into their own entities, and may — as they reach age 9 or 10 — question their own parents' infallibility. Let the fun begin!

Creating a Legacy

What legacy do we really want to leave our kids? This is the most important question for us as parents and as our children begin to develop their own individual personalities complete with values, talents and quirks. What kind of adults do we want our children to become?

Think of a list for your own children. The list we created may be different from yours, but here it is. We were determined that our children would grow up to:

1. Be physically healthy.
2. Be happy.
3. Be generous, kind, and sharing.
4. Respect and nourish the people in their lives and the earth they lived on.
5. Have a continuing joy of learning.
6. Have the intellectual and emotional tools to see the "big picture." (The more choices and options they could imagine, the more choices they would have to solve the problems confronting them.)

What's missing in our list? There's no mention of a wonderful mate, wealth, success, and so on. We were certain that the six wishes we picked would lead to all other positive outcomes. These six characteristics were the foundation of ultimate joy and happiness in their lives. The laws of Cause and Effect and Fulfillment are immutable and timeless.

Cause and Effect: The Ultimate, Infallible Rule

Take advantage of the fact that between the ages of 6 and 9, children positively adore rules and rituals.

> *Kids at this age see the world in black and white, and use rules to help them interpret what is right and wrong.*

Now is a critical opportunity to drive home the vital principle of Cause and Effect and its relationship to Fulfillment. The earlier you can get the Perfect System into your kids, the better. Your children are blank slates while in their early cognitive years. For obvious reasons, it is easier to teach fresh behaviour skills when you don't have to erase bad behaviour habits first.

- For every action, there is an equal and opposite reaction.
- Positive actions beget positive reactions; negative actions beget negative reactions.
- We are responsible for what happens to us in our lives.

Teach it to your children — and teach it to them again. Then teach it over and over again. Drum it into them until they live and breathe this truth. It is the most critical and valuable lesson you can ever teach them.

Our ignorance of this truth is creating misery that deepens like an ocean shelf, worse for each successive generation. It is the reason why courses in "crisis mediation" and "conflict resolution" are quickly becoming necessary in today's school system. Teachers are reporting that antisocial behaviour in their classrooms has reached epidemic proportions — and a class that is unruly is a class that is unproductive. A class that is unruly is also a potential hotbed of racism, sexism, and other forms of intolerance.

In the lower grades we teach our children the arts, the sciences, and the basic learning tools of reading and writing, yet we utterly ignore what is both our greatest responsibility and our greatest opportunity: to influence our children wisely before their misbehaviour escalates and requires crisis management. Teachers are also victimized by this reality. The stresses and frustrations that arise from having to deal with this issue are the major causes of teacher burnout.

How to explain Cause and Effect

Take advantage of your child's rapidly increasing verbal and cognitive abilities, from about the age of 7 onward, by clearly articulating and discussing the Law of Cause and Effect.

I (Ellen) teach a course to groups of children. Here's how I help them understand the concept of Cause and Effect. You will want to use your own words, but you will find some helpful tips here to introduce your own children to the principle.

Typically, I begin by asking one of the children to stand up and talk to me just like their "worst enemy" might talk to them in the schoolyard. When the student has done this, I ask all the children to talk about how they felt about the kid who was mouthing off. Then I ask them how they felt about the person who was receiving the hurtful words. The kids' comments are all written on the board.

From there, I line up a row of dominoes and set them in motion.

I explain that the "neat" action they are watching is due to a principle called Cause and Effect.

"What does it mean?" I ask, and then explain: "Everything is affected by something. The first domino is called a *cause*, and the next one is called the *effect*.

"Usually, we hate it when we are just an effect. Why? Because we feel we don't have any control over our life. It seems that life or people and teachers and kids are doing things to us and we have to react — things like making us do homework, or hollering at us, or punishing us for something we didn't do. It stinks just being an effect. Do you ever feel like you're just an effect?"

This leads to a great discussion. Children love to talk about being put upon. At this point, I say to the class: "The question is, are you really only an *effect*? Did that kid holler at you for no reason? Did you get more homework than usual because of something you did or didn't do? And the consequence for the bad deed you didn't do — why didn't they believe you? The answer, and this is going to be difficult to understand, is that where there is an *effect*, there must always be a *cause*."

We used this exercise at home, too. Ask your child to think about — and talk about — possible reasons behind other people's actions. "So let's be honest. Why did that kid holler at you? Why did he or she feel able to communicate to you in that manner? Three possible reasons! One is that you may have made him or her angry at you some other time — maybe not at that very moment but a few days ago. Another reason might be that by not saying anything to that person about how you wish to be talked to, your silence (an action nonetheless) allowed that person to treat you like a dirt bag. Not standing up for yourself or for someone else is an action, too. The third reason might be that the cause has nothing to do with you but with something else in the other person's life." This is a great opportunity to discuss and teach the concept of empathy.

If reason one or two are in play, the important thing is to get your child thinking about the fact that what he or she did or said — or didn't say or do — to another kid at some point is likely what caused the kid to react the way he or she did. Make the point that maybe your child didn't do it at that very moment, but that at some point, their actions are responsible. Use your own words to say something like this: "Whenever something happens to you, ask yourself the question, 'Who's responsible?' This is the hardest lesson to learn: We can control almost everything that happens to us either by something we do or don't do."

At this stage in the discussion, it's very important to clarify that a few things in life are unfortunately out of a child's control — for example, if the child gets sick, or some accident happens to someone they know. Point out that things like this are not in the child's control, but most things are.

> When it comes to things that are in the child's control, they have no one to blame but themselves for what happens.

Say something like: "I know it feels easier to blame other people, but it's your actions that affect what happens to you. Stop and think before you act — and especially before you react."

At this point, use three dominoes to make the case that the central domino can be both a *cause* and an *effect*. Explain that at any point they can be a cause or an effect; it is their choice.

Now back to Ellen's classroom role play.

I tell kids that the more they understand this idea, the more powerful they will become. I liken it to becoming a Superhero. I finish off by tapping into children's current fondness for rules. "And what's great about this Cause and Effect stuff," I tell them, "is that there are simple rules to follow, so you don't have to make it up as you go along. The rules are the rules!"

Point out Cause and Effect in action

Kids are very literal at this stage, so look for ways to tangibly demonstrate the impact of Cause and Effect and support its truth. Integrate its principles into every aspect of your lives together.

- For every action, there is an equal and opposite reaction.
- Negative actions beget negative reactions.
- Positive actions beget positive reactions.

Look for every opportunity to reinforce the message. Watch nature programs and read nature books, and point out how Cause and Effect is the law that governs our entire existence on this planet.

On the sports field, talk about what happens when players put their own desires above those of the team. Discuss what would happen to the team if there were no rules. Point out that by pulling together and putting other team members' needs ahead of their own, each member of the team ensures that the team pulls ahead.

Teach Children to Care — and to Share

Build empathy in your children and encourage the concept of putting others first. You can do this by helping them imagine themselves in another person's situation. Ask them to think about why their friends — and especially those who aren't their friends — act the way they do. Do they come from an unhappy home? Is this a stressful time in their lives? Do they have trouble keeping up in class? Are they shy or scared? Feeling hurt? Feeling ignored?

> *The key is to get your child thinking about other people – and about how other people may be feeling.*

Encourage your child to try an experiment for the day. Kids love experiments. Instruct him or her to try sharing for a day and see what happens — to try putting another person's needs before their own. To sweep the floor without being asked. To share a treat with a friend without being asked. To ask someone how they are feeling. Your child will be truly surprised by the *effect*. It's funny: People react in the strangest ways when they feel that you care about them.

Point out that it's not going to be easy, because all of us instinctively want to take care of ourselves first. Learning to share is a skill we have to learn. However, the more we practice it, the easier it becomes.

Forbid verbal putdowns

We have discussed how your child's cognitive and verbal abilities become increasingly sophisticated between the ages of 6 and 9. In many kids, this new-found ability, while it has many advantages, also leads to something unfortunate: the discovery of verbal putdowns of friends and family members — possibly even including you as parents.

Ask your child to think about how they would feel if they were at the receiving end of hurtful verbal behaviour. Point out that words can be just as abusive as hitting or kicking.

> *Hurtful behaviour of any kind goes against the rules and values of the house and is not acceptable.*

If the inappropriate behaviour is repeated, use the three-choices rule:

Choice #1: You will immediately stop the hurtful behaviour and apologize to the other child or family member.

Choice #2: Or you will go to your room and stay there until you are ready to follow the rules of the house and apologize to the other child or family member.

Choice #3: Or I will take you to your room and you will stay there until you are ready to follow the rules of the house and apologize to the other child or family member.

Be Your Child's Media Monitor

Many children pick up the habit of verbally abusing others from watching TV or inappropriate movies. Make no mistake about it — when we allow children of this age to watch TV, surf online, read inappropriate comic books, or scour newspapers unsupervised, we are abdicating our parental responsibility.

> **You MUST monitor all the media that your child is exposed to!**

The media are an extremely powerful force that can be used for both positive and negative purposes. Even as adults, it is not always easy for us to discern which is which. Without constant and conscious awareness, we are all too frequently manipulated into accepting inaccurate or erroneous points of view, or buying into false perceptions of people or the world at large.

It is one of the reasons why the Law of Cause and Effect is not given its proper focus in society and in education. The media constantly show people or organizations that seem to succeed, despite a pattern of negative action or self-obsession. We don't see the connection between positive action and positive results, because this is not the stuff that high TV ratings are made of. Instead, time and again we see the bad guy triumphing, and pages and pages in print and online devoted to those who make it their goal to float aimlessly through life. Surely this is not the way we want our children to view the world.

That said, there is conversely some wonderful, stimulating content on TV, in print, and online that can open up worlds of inspiration and information for our children. The key is to ensure that this is what your child is exposed to.

However, you cannot ensure this when you allow a young child unsupervised media or computer access. As a parent, you must instead become your child's 24/7 media monitor. Record educational programs on nature, travel, history, visual arts, and the performing arts, together with quality children's programs, classic dramas, and appropriate films and sporting events. Rent movies, DVDs, and CDs from the store or borrow them from the library. When your child wants to watch TV, you will have a catalogue of appropriate and entertaining material ready for viewing. If asked, explain why you are acting as their "media police." This opportunity will then prepare them to self-regulate and understand their level of readiness to pick what they view.

Use filtering software to restrict your child's online adventures to just a few sites that you have carefully vetted. And be sure to keep the computer in the main family area. Never let your child have access to it when you are not around.

One final point to mention here. Unfortunately, many of your child's friends' parents will not be nearly as vigilant as they should be about the media their children are exposed to. When your child is going to another home for a sleepover, call the parents and let them know how carefully you monitor your child's media viewing. Tell them your child will bring along a selection of child-appropriate DVDs for the evening unless the parents have other plans.

You possibly will get pushback from parents who are not aware of the Perfect System. This presents a wonderful opportunity for an open discussion about the Perfect System of Parenting. We accepted the fact, at the beginning of our parenthood, that many of the parents our children would come into contact with would not subscribe to our rigorous view of parenting. When the opportunity arose, this state of affairs was openly discussed with our kids. It taught them to understand that different people have different ways of raising their children. None was better, none worse. However, ours was non-negotiable because it was *ours*. These situations became "teaching moments" for our kids — opportunities for us to retell our Perfect System philosophy.

Undoing a Love-ambushed Relationship

"I don't love you anymore." The five most painful words for a parent to hear. What to do when you find yourself caught in the love ambush? Here, in sequence, is how we responded when it happened to us.

1. We did not let our child see that this killer statement affected us emotionally.
2. We stated clearly that he must stop the negative action that led up to the killer statement.
3. We then responded with the one disarming statement guaranteed to end any negative behavioural spiral. We looked the child straight in the eye and said, "I'm sorry to hear that, but it does not change my job." It took a great deal of courage to say this, but we felt this was the way to nip this problem in the bud.
4. We continued by explaining slowly and coolly that *our* job was to love *him*. Whether *he* loved *us* or not was not part of our job. It would be nice if he felt that way, but what we really wanted was for him to be a kind and sharing person. We reinforced that "this is the kind of person we want to be around and this is the kind of person the world needs right now."
5. We then reiterated that our job was to be his teacher and protector. "Mommy and Daddy are the people who try and make sure that nothing bad will happen to you," we said,

"because we want you to be a happy boy."
6. We then asked if what we said was clear. If not, we would calmly repeat it. Once our son understood the message, or the fact that we would not budge from ours, we then asked him to stop the goofy behaviour that instigated the lesson.
7. If he did not stop, we then went into our three-choices scenario.

Making the Teacher Your Partner

When our children entered school at the junior-kindergarten level, we immediately tried to create partnership with their teachers. It was obvious from the start that most teachers do not have the basic Cause and Effect teaching skills and knowledge. With both of our kids' teachers, we gingerly started a dialogue to explain our philosophy. We didn't want to appear too aggressive and thus elicit the wrong response. We wanted their partnership.

In today's schools, teachers are hip to civics and ethics. To our minds, the principle of Cause and Effect supersedes ethics. Ethics implies appropriate societal behaviour to others. However, the principles of Cause and Effect are more elemental — more to the point. Whereas ethics is about behaviour to others, Cause and Effect is about behaviour to oneself. It is a behaviour methodology that is also a tool for fulfillment and happiness — ultimately for oneself, but also for others, by definition: What is best for oneself is to continuously be in a sharing mindset, taking care of the other person. It is ethics in reverse.

Furthermore, ethics is a theoretical philosophy while the Perfect System is a practical, everyday, hit-the-road way of living.

Frankly, our goal of partnership with the school was not universally successful. It worked with one of our kids' teachers, but not the other. The supportive teacher wanted to know more and asked for more details, so we gave her the Perfect System principles. This led to more conversation, and eventually she became a true partner. She gladly reported to us weekly, or even more frequently if the situation demanded. Most importantly, she supported our thinking in the way she dealt with our son — not the entire class, but our child. She felt that this methodology could be taught systemically in the classroom only when it was being reinforced at home with all the students. Otherwise the children would be getting mixed signals and the ensuing confusion would not be good for them. This teacher was a delight, and so was our first child's early schooling.

The response of our other son's teacher was antithetical to this. Basically, she didn't get it and only paid lip-service to our request. So we went into protective mode — code red. His early schooling was difficult for us because we had to keep explaining and reinforcing our point of view whenever he returned from school. It is interesting to note that it was obvious and clear to our son that his school environment did not respect the rules of the Perfect System. This confused him at first, but it proved to be a blessing in disguise because he came to see the chaos and anarchy that reigned when the rules of the Perfect System were not put into practice. He was a model kid at home because he was in an environment that he could control.

Ages 6 to 9: Key Messages Recapped
- From age 7 onward, begin to clearly articulate and discuss the theory and principles of Cause and Effect. Drive home the basic message over and over again.
- Teach that verbal putdowns are as bad as physical abuse

and are not acceptable. Contain such behaviour using the three-choices rule.
- Undo a love ambush by negating the power of a child's killer statement, "I don't love you." Make it clear that this has no impact on you. Reiterate that your job is not to gain your child's love, but rather to protect and love him or her.
- Encourage children to put themselves in other people's shoes. Encourage sharing.
- Monitor all the media that your child is exposed to.
- Initiate an open dialogue with your child's teacher regarding your Cause and Effect philosophy. Avoid being aggressive; tread gently. If interest is shown, you may find it helpful to lend this book to the teacher.
- Be prepared, if the teacher is unsupportive, to keep explaining and reinforcing your point of view with your child.

8

From 10 to 13

These years have been called the make-or-break years. There is certainly some basis for this description. As kids move from these "tween" years into the teen years, unchecked behaviour will only get worse and it will become very difficult to change poor attitudes and habits.

Although it's not always easy to undo poor behavioural patterns in the tween years either, it is easier to do so during these years.

But let's start with the premise that you've been following the Perfect System of Parenting all along, in which case your primary goal will be to ensure that your great kid continues along the path you've laid and turns into an equally wonderful teenager.

> *Recognize that although your son or daughter's peers are becoming increasingly important to them, you still have enormous and important influence on them.*

But your influence won't last forever. Now is the time to establish fundamental expectations and limits for the upcoming teen years, and cement existing values and house rules. Continually reinforce the fundamental Law of Cause and Effect. You'll reap the benefits many times over in years to come.

Know What You're Up Against

Kids in the tween years are going through phenomenal physical changes, including at the hormone and brain chemistry levels. A roiling mixture of hormones and emotions, they slip back and forth between good days and bad days.

Kids of this age also slip back and forth in terms of childish behaviour versus grown-up behaviour. Some days they want your comfort and affection; the next day they may fear this is a childish need and unconsciously push you away.

Let your kids know that you understand that they are going through a period of change as they start to mature, but be firm about the need to uphold house values such as courtesy and consideration for others in the family.

Establish Priorities

It is important for you to reassess the rules that guide your children's behaviour as they move through the tween years. Your most important responsibility as parents is to help prepare your children for independent lives as adults, which means allowing them increasing independence as they grow older. However, their protection remains of paramount importance. You must strive to keep them out of harm's way by establishing or upholding rules that safeguard them from harmful behaviour. This means easing up on the number of rules, but being one hundred percent firm about enforcing the rules and values that you consider critical for their well-being and the family's happiness.

When it comes to setting priorities, you may want to differentiate between things that you find mildly irritating and things that are significant. For example, while you may be irritated by outlandish or garish clothing, consider whether your child's well-being or safety is really being compromised. If not, perhaps you can live with your child's temporarily poor fashion sense in exchange for his or her adherence to rules that relate to values or safety.

Remember the parenting guideline established in chapter 3 of always asking the question, What good will my next action do for my child? If it does *no good* for your child, then that's what you'll eventually get back — *no good*. This philosophy makes an excellent foundation for setting rules throughout childhood and through the tween and teen years. Use it to help establish the rules you consider critical.

You may also find this guideline helpful when your child comes to you with the inevitable plaintive whine: "But everyone else is allowed to do this. All the other parents allow it." Point out to your child that your responsibility as a parent does not include winning "popular parent" contests or copying what other parents do. Your responsibility is to keep your child out of harm's way and to protect his or her future happiness the best way you know. That is why the rules you establish must be upheld.

As discussed earlier in the book, if you decide that some rules are no longer relevant or necessary, don't just let them slip. This suggests that the rules weren't meaningful or important in the first place. And it takes credibility away from the remaining rules. Instead, talk about why certain rules are no longer required, and explain why others must remain or be newly introduced. Stress that the rules that are in place are not negotiable.

Offer Kids More Choices

Kids of this age often go through a "gimme" stage. They want electronic toys, brand-name clothing, and increasing freedom to go to movies or other events with their friends. As parents, we cannot — and must not — give our children everything they ask for. But we can find safe ways to give them more freedom to make their own choices.

For example, instead of paying for everything your child needs, consider coming up with a monthly allowance to cover all expenses. Draw up a budget with your tween that covers everything from clothing and movies to gifts, school supplies, and charitable donations.

This is a good time to give your tween some elementary budgeting lessons. Suggest that he or she divide up the monthly allowance into specific sections such as "needs," "wants," "savings," and "charity." We recommend that you establish a rule that at least ten percent must go to a charitable cause. Reinforce the message that giving to others is the ultimate source of true fulfillment.

Let tweens make their own choices about purchases made, but stress that they must make the allowance stretch for the entire month. Let them know that you won't be helping out, even if the piggy bank is totally empty. This not only gives children the independence of more choices, it also reinforces the fundamental truth of Cause and Effect: if they make poor choices at the start of the month, there will be no cash left at the end of the month.

Let Your Child Experience Consequences

As you give your children more independence, make it clear that in return you expect them to assume more responsibility for their actions. For example, if a young child leaves a prized possession outside in the garden, most parents will ensure that the child brings it in before it gets lost or damaged. However, if your tween continually leaves an electronic toy in the garden, the day it becomes soaked in the rain and ceases to work is a day for reinforcing the Law of Cause and Effect.

> *Keep protecting your child physically; stop protecting your child from the consequences of his or her negligence or mistakes.*

Yes, it is hard to stand by and watch your child stumble, but making mistakes is an important part of growing up for them. Consequences are an amazing teacher.

Handling Negative Behaviour

As children struggle to cross the bridge from childhood to the teen years, many lash out at their parents and become openly confrontational. Others revert to passive aggression, becoming sullen or quietly sarcastic. Your previously delightful child may appear to be turning into a monster, arguing against your opinions and questioning your every rule.

It is time to sit down with your child and review the rules and culture of the house. Reinforce the concept of the family hierarchy: your child is not the most important member; your child does not come first. Reinforce the concept that this family believes in others coming before oneself. Acknowledge that your child is growing up and developing independent interests and opinions, and let him or her know that you will always be interested to hear these opinions and points of view, although you may not agree with them. Make it clear that you have expectations. You expect the same respect from your child for other family members' opinions and beliefs. State very firmly that confrontational or otherwise discourteous behaviour will not be tolerated in the house. Discuss the consequences of breaking this rule. At this stage, your child may be able to choose an alternative form of expression.

Establish a Parent-Child Contract

Contracts can be a valuable way to agree on and uphold rules and household expectations, together with consequences for broken rules and rewards for good behaviour. A good contract is also a very practical illustration of Cause and Effect in action.

Your contract should be the result of discussion between you and your child. It will include rules, curfews, and chores. Be very specific about expectations. For example, don't say, "Come home early on school days." This leaves room for interpretation. Instead, specify the time your child is expected to be home.

Ask your child to suggest consequences for each rule not upheld. These might range from no TV or computer game time to not being allowed out with friends for an agreed-upon period of time. Get your child to draft the final contract, which should then be signed by both you and your child and kept in a safe place.

Keep the Lines of Communication Open

When kids are little, they love to chat with you about anything and everything. But as they reach the tween years, many become downright cagey about what is going on in their lives. When this happens, your first instinct as a parent will probably be to suspect the worst: that something must be wrong, that there is something your child doesn't want you to know.

Be aware that this probably isn't the case. It's quite normal for kids to start zealously guarding their privacy — both physically and emotionally — between the ages of 10 and 13. They share feelings and secrets with their friends, but are often loath to let you in.

That said, it's important for you to keep communication lines as open as you possibly can. Open communication will be your greatest ally when your tween becomes a teen, so make extra efforts to chat on a regular basis. Look for non-threatening, non-confrontational opportunities to initiate conversation about your child's life, feelings, and friends. Some kids of this age find it difficult to make eye contact when talking, so look for opportunities to chat when you are side by side and your child can't get away — for example, when you are stuck in a traffic jam or out walking in the park.

Also watch for signals that your child wants to initiate discussion with you. Such signals may not necessarily be verbal. For example, if your child suddenly starts hanging around you while you're cooking or catching up with work, it may mean that he or she wants to chat. These opportunities don't come up very often. If at all possible, stop what you're doing and listen actively. Show that you are there for your child and want to listen. There's an old adage: You have two ears and one mouth; use them in that proportion. In short, as the parent of tweens or teens, it often pays to listen more than you talk.

Ages 10 to 13: Key Messages Recapped

- You still have significant influence over your child. Establish and reinforce a solid foundation of limits and expectations while you have the chance.
- Ease up on the number of rules; be vigilant about upholding the rules that you consider critical.
- In return for granting increased independence, expect your child to assume greater responsibility for his or her behaviour and for household help.
- Give your child safe ways to make more choices.
- Protect your child physically, but stop protecting your child from the consequences of his or her own negligence or mistakes.
- Reinforce the family hierarchy: Your child does not come first.

- Clearly communicate that confrontational or otherwise antisocial behaviour will not be tolerated.
- Develop and sign a written parent-child contract.
- Keep communication lines open.

9

14 and Beyond

Hold on tight — you could be in for a rocky ride! Even the best behaved kids tend to go through some challenging stages during the teen years. Parents are in for a major challenge if their kids have come through childhood with entrenched negative attitudes and habits. It is extremely difficult to change bad behaviour once kids get into their teens. Note that we said "difficult," not "impossible." Further on in this chapter, we will give you an example of how one of us helped one set of parents turn the corner with a seemingly very troubled teen.

Teen Characteristics

Let's start with the assumption that your kid isn't a particularly difficult kid, just a normally "sometimes difficult" teen. If so, your teen may well portray at least one or two of the following characteristics. Your teen may be:

- Hyper-sensitive
- Self-conscious
- Self-critical
- Obsessed with self
- Critical of you
- Sarcastic
- Argumentative
- Rebellious
- Intensely private
- Thoughtless

Many teens are also driven by a fierce search for fulfillment, which can lead to risky behaviour in a variety of areas: alcohol, drugs, sex, partying, gambling, driving, and so on. Please note that the abstract concept of fulfillment is a key part of the Perfect System. It is essential, therefore, that you discuss, whenever appropriate, this idea with your teen. Your teen is at the developmental stage where it is possible that he or she will grasp it. The *it* is the difference between a quick fix — instantaneous self gratification — and long-lasting fulfillment. Your teen is inundated with fast cars, sex, drugs, etc. This negative noise surrounds them. They hear it from their friends, their peers, and in every part of the media.

You have a big job as a parent now. You have to teach the Perfect System to your teen. Please review the basic principles laid out in chapter 2.

Try to find an opportunity to discuss the Perfect System non-confrontationally during the early teen years — hopefully before any risky behaviour has started. For example, use a newspaper or TV report about an incident to initiate conversation. As kids move through their teens, their capacity for abstract thought increases. Many will enjoy philosophical discussion and debate. Use this to your advantage to get important Perfect System messages across.

Be prepared for the fact that your teen at times may appear to be irritated by you or may even seem to actively dislike you. Teens are trying to shed their childhood identity, and your mere existence as a parent makes you an obstacle to this. Don't take it personally — your loving son or daughter will return one day. (Maybe as soon as next week for a day or two, given teen mood swings.) But don't accept bad behaviour either. There can be no give-me's with a teen. If a teen screws up, there must be immediate sanction and action.

When talking to a teen who has acted out, stay detached, unemotional, and calm. Make it clear that a display of love or affection is not required from him or her and is of no real consequence to you, but that respect — human dignity — is always demanded.

> *Remind yourself that your primary job as a parent is not to be liked or to receive love.*

Tough love is painful for a parent but is essential for the teen's welfare and future happiness.

Don't Solve Your Teen's Problems

Most teens thoroughly resent it when parents try to solve their problems for them. Being overprotective of teens is also no way to help them become productive adults. Making mistakes and feeling disappointment and pain are all an essential part of growing up. Besides, it is also the only way for teens to learn the real truth of Cause and Effect.

Be there as coach and sounding board, but let teens come up with their own solutions to everyday problems. Share information and experience, but guide them to take ownership of issues and solutions. This will help them develop their judgment and sense of personal responsibility. Walk beside your teen — don't try to carry him or her.

> *Think of yourself as an objective counsellor, encouraging your teen to think through options and develop solutions.*

Not all your teen's solutions will work, of course, but this too is an important lesson. Teens need to make their own mistakes in order to begin to learn from the consequences. They must learn first-hand that they are the cause of the effect that follows.

Turning Bad Behaviour Around

As we have already stated, it is very difficult to change behaviour once children get into their teens, but it's not impossible. One of us counselled the parents of a very difficult, troubled teenage girl who ultimately reported very positive results. Let us share with you precisely what happened as these parents started using the Perfect System.

After a behavioural blowup by the teen, the parents sat down with her. They admitted failure for their past methods of behavioural control and apologized. They explained that they had done the best they could with the information they had — namely, what they had picked up from their parents or friends and had read in parenting books. However, they acknowledged that this old method or philosophy was clearly not working, because they could see how unhappy she was.

They went on to assure their daughter that her happiness was everything to them, and the unavoidable truth was that through no conscious fault of their own, in their own minds, they had partially failed as parents.

You better believe they had their teen's attention by this point!

The couple then began a dialogue with their daughter about the Perfect System of Parenting, introducing fundamental concepts such as Cause and Effect, the Love Ambush, and so on. This took a number of conversations; the parents had to pick their moments. Eventually, their teen bought in to the system.

Once she was onside, the parents developed a Partnership Agreement with her. Just like the parent-child contracts we recommended in the last chapter, this agreement included an actual written agreement that needed to be signed by all parties. Importantly, the agreement was co-authored by the parents and the teen.

The agreement clearly laid out the rules (expectations), and the consequences and rewards for breaking or abiding by the agreement. The three-count consequence used with younger children was clearly not appropriate, so the parents and teen drew up a selected list of consequences, including:

- No TV for a specified time

- No computer for a specified time
- Being grounded at home for a specified time
- No cell phone for a specified time

On the reward side, the agreement included such items as:

- More unsupervised time outside the home
- More car time
- Later curfew at night
- Private cell phone

As part of the agreement, it was determined that if the teen broke the agreement, they would all sit down and decide together what the appropriate response or consequence should be. At this point, the parents would sit down calmly with the teen and ask, "What would you do in our place?" They would then prompt their daughter to role-play. Of course, the teen always picked the least harsh of the possible consequences, but the lessons learned through this process were phenomenal. Here they are:

1. The teen was able to empathize with the parents' dilemma and the parents' point of view.
2. The teen was learning to take responsibility for her misbehaviour.
3. The teen was learning that she couldn't continue to get away with the bad behaviour that had provoked the new negotiated contract.

The parents reported great changes in their child. One of the most gratifying was that due to her new understanding of Cause and

Effect, she had started to do helpful things around the house without being asked. Why? Because she understood the concept that doing good results in getting good back.

> **Ages 14 and Over: Key Messages Recapped**
> - Before issues arise, talk to your teen about the link between the search for fulfillment and risky behaviour.
> - Take advantage of your teen's increasing capacity for abstract thought to discuss important messages from the Perfect System.
> - If a teen screws up, there must be immediate sanction and action. Stay calm, quiet, and unemotional when discussing unacceptable behaviour.
> - Don't try to solve all your teen's problems. Coach and guide your teen to take ownership of issues and solutions. Let teens learn from their mistakes.
> - Co-draft a Partnership Agreement to be signed by all parties. Agree on the possible consequences and rewards.
> - When kids break the agreement, ask them what they would do in your situation. Ask them to select an appropriate consequence.
> - Don't expect your teen's negative behavioural habits to change overnight. It will take time.

We won't pretend that all of this happened overnight. There were years of bad parenting to overcome, so the turnaround took time. But there was a turnaround. A very troubled and unsettled household became much less stressful. And the change was lasting.

Conclusion

The Big Bang. Cause and Effect. Fulfillment. Containment. Throughout this book we have used these and other scientific principles to elucidate and illustrate what we have called the Perfect System of Parenting. In addition, we have given you parenting tips and strategies. And we have talked about who is in charge and the number-one responsibility of parents to keep their children safe.

Basing parenting on scientific truths could seem a little mechanical or pragmatic to some.

But nothing could be further from our purposes — or from the way the universe works! As you will see when you begin to live by these principles in your home, they are part of the sheer poetry of life. Imagine this: Every relationship in your home, every aspect of the life of your home, can be intimately connected to the essential

Conclusion

principles of life itself — this life of incredible power and beauty all around us.

We believe you will find that by following the Perfect System of Parenting, your home will be one where all are safe to love and laugh and live in joy — together.

For Further Reading

Books

What to Expect: The First Year, Heidi E. Murkoff, Arlene Eisenberg, and Sandee E. Hathaway, Workman Publishing, 1996.
What to Expect: The Toddler Years, Arlene Eisenberg, Heidi E. Murkoff, and Sandee E. Hathaway, Workman Publishing, 1994.
Your Baby and Child: From Birth to Age 5, rev. ed., Penelope Leach, Alfred A. Knopf, 1997.
Raising Great Kids: Ages 6 to 12: The Complete Guide to Your Child's Health and Development, edited by Christine Langlois, Ballantine Books, 1999. (In collaboration with the Canadian Paediatric Society and the College of Family Physicians of Canada.)
Understanding Your Teen: Ages 13 to 19, edited by Christine Langlois, Ballantine Books, 1999. (In collaboration with the Canadian Paediatric Society and the College of Family Physicians of Canada.)

For Further Reading

Online

www.canadianparents.com
www.todaysparent.com
www.whattoexpect.com
http://parenting.ivillage.com/
www.raisingkids.co.uk
http://www.bbc.co.uk/parenting/
http://www.cich.ca/index_eng.html
   (Canadian Institute of Child Health)
www.pampers.com

www.ingramcontent.com/pod-product-compliance
Lightning Source LLC
Chambersburg PA
CBHW060402080526
44583CB00012B/433